J. DOBRZYŃSKI TEXT | PHOTOS J. DOBR... / A. BUKOWSKI / STRATUS COLL.

Polish Aviation Museum
Cracow

STRATUS

© 2010 Jarosław Dobrzyński
© 2010 Mushroom Model Publications

Published in Poland in 2010
by STRATUS s.c.
Po. Box 123,
27-600 Sandomierz 1, Poland
e-mail: office@mmpbooks.biz
for
Mushroom Model Publications,
3 Gloucester Close, Petersfield,
Hampshire GU32 3AX, UK.
e-mail: rogerw@mmpbooks.biz
http://www.mmpbooks.biz

All rights reserved. Apart from any fair dealing for the purpose of private study, research, criticism or review, as permitted under the Copyright, Design and Patents Act, 1988, no part of this publication may be reproduced, stored in a retrieval system, or transmitted in any form or by any means, electronic, electrical, chemical, mechanical, optical, photocopying, recording or otherwise, without prior written permission. All enquiries should be addressed to the publisher.

**ISBN
978-83-61421-03-0**

Editor in chief
Roger Wallsgrove

Editorial Team
Bartłomiej Belcarz
Robert Pęczkowski
Artur Juszczak

Translation
Jarosław Dobrzyński

Proof reading
Roger Wallsgrove

Layout Concept
Bartłomiej Belcarz
Artur Bukowski

Photos
Jarosław Dobrzyński
Artur Bukowski
Dariusz Karnas
Bartłomiej Belcarz
Artur Juszczak
Robert Pęczkowski

Printed by
Drukarnia Diecezjalna,
ul. Żeromskiego 4, 27-600 Sandomierz
tel. +48 (15) 832 31 92, fax +48 (15) 832 77 87
www.wds.pl, marketing@wds.pl
PRINTED IN POLAND

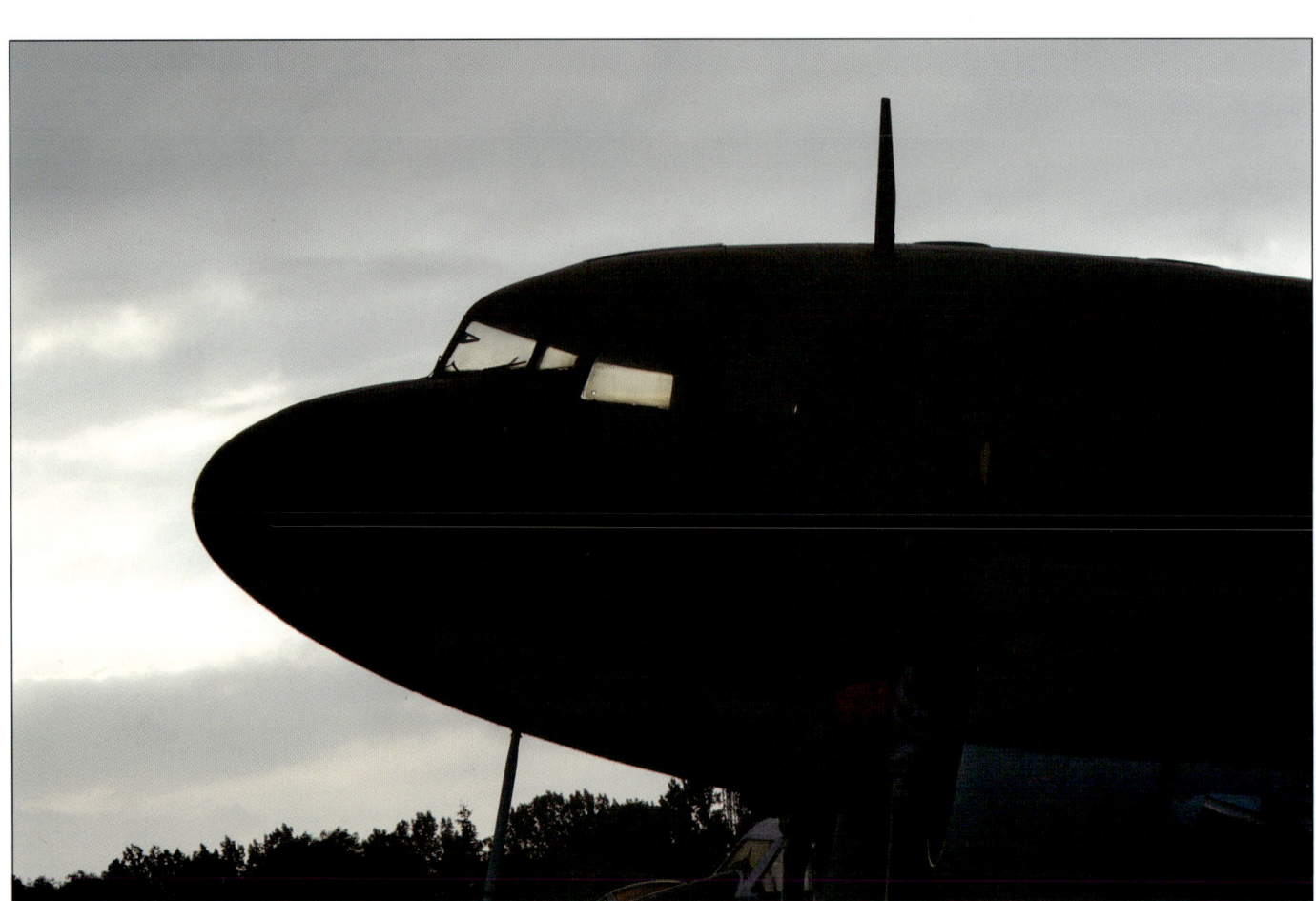

Contents

History 5

The new building 8

Chapter 1: The Small Hangar 10

Albatros B.IIa. 12	Albatros H.1. 16	Sopwith F1 Camel. 20
DFW C.V. 13	Aviatik C.III. 17	Grigorovich M-15 21
LFG Roland D.VIb. 14	LVG B.II. 18	
Albatros C.I. 15	Halberstadt Cl.II 19	

Chapter 2: 1930s to the present 22

RWD-13. 24	Yakovlev Yak-17UTI 44	SZD-18 *Czajka*. 59
RWD-21. 25	Yakovlev Yak-23. 45	IS-B *Komar* 49 60
PZL P.11c. 26	Avia B-33 46	IS-4 *Jastrząb* 60
PWS-26 28	Zlin Z-26 *Trener* 47	SZD-6X *Nietoperz*. 61
Curtiss Hawk II 29	Aero-145 48	SZD-9*bis Bocian* 1A 61
TS-9 *Junak* 3 30	Aero L-60E *Brigadyr* 49	IS-C *Żuraw* 62
TS-8 *Bies* 31	Aero L-200A *Morava* 50	SZD-10*bis Czapla* 62
Kukułka (Cuckoo) 32	Bücker Bü-131 *Jungmann* 51	SZD-8*bis Jaskółka* 63
Piper L-4A Grasshopper 33	Messerschmitt Bf 109G. 52	SZD –17X *Jaskółka L.* 63
North American T-6G Texan 34	SP-GIL. 53	SZD-12 *Mucha* 100 64
Cessna UC-78A Bobcat 35	JK-1 *Trzmiel*. 54	SZD-22C *Mucha* Standard . . 64
De Havilland DH-82A Tiger Moth . 36	SM-1 54	SZD-15 *Sroka*. 65
Supermarine Spitfire LF Mk XVIe. . 37	SM-2 55	SZD-21-2B *Kobuz* 3 65
Polikarpov Po-2 LNB. 39	Mil Mi-2URP. 56	SZD-25A *Lis* 66
Tupolev Tu-2S 40	WWS *Wrona bis* 57	SZD-19-2A *Zefir* 2A. 66
Yakovlev Yak-11. 41	WWS-2 *Żaba* 58	SZD-43 *Orion* 67
Yakovlev Yak-12. 42	IS-A *Salamandra* 58	Swift S-1 67
Yakovlev Yak-18. 43	IS-1 *Sęp bis* 59	

Chapter 3: The open air exhibition and MiG Alley 69

Lim-1. 70	MiG-21U 83	Cessna A-37B Dragonfly 98
Lim–2 71	Mikoyan MiG-21 bis. 83	Lockheed F-104S Starfighter 99
MiG-15UTI 72	MiG-21US 84	Dassault Mirage 5BA. 100
SB Lim-2 73	MiG-21UM 84	Ling Temco Vought A-7P Corsair II 101
SB Lim-2A 74	Mikoyan MiG-23MF 85	Lisunov Li-2 102
Lim-5 75	Mikoyan MiG-29UB 86	Ilyushin (VEB) Il-14S. 104
Lim-6bis 76	Ilyushin Il-28R/S-Il-28 87	Yakovlev Yak-40 105
Lim-6MR. 77	PZL TS-11 *Iskra* 88	SEPECAT Jaguar GR.1. 106
Mikoyan MiG-19PM 78	Sukhoi Su-7BM 89	Fouga CM.170 *Magister* 107
Mikoyan MiG-21. 79	Sukhoi Su-7BKL 90	Mil Mi-4 108
Mikoyan MiG-21F13. 79	Sukhoi Su-7U. 91	Mil Mi-8 109
Mikoyan MiG-21PF. 79	Sukhoi Su-20 92	Sud-Aviation SA-3160 *Alouette* III 110
Mikoyan MiG-21PFM 80	Sukhoi Su-22 93	Bell CH-136 Kiowa 111
Mikoyan MiG-21MF. 80	Republic F-84F Thunderstreak 94	Tupolev Tu-134A 112
Mikoyan MiG-21M 81	SAAB J35J *Draken*. 95	PZL M-15 *Belfegor* 113
Mikoyan MiG-21R 81	SAAB AJSF 37 *Viggen* 96	
MiG-21 - the Fourth Generation . . 82	Northrop F-5E Tiger II 97	

Chapter 4: You don't know your own – the stories of history 115

Levavasseur Antoinette 116	AEG Wagner *Eule* 120	LWD *Żuraw*. 122
Friedrich Etrich *Taube*. 117	Geest *Moewe* IV 120	BŻ-4 *Żuk* (Beetle) 122
Heinkel He-5f 118	Albatros L.101 121	HWL *Pegaz* 123
Messerschmitt Me 209 V1 119	LWD *Szpak* 2. 121	Zeppelin Staaken R.VI bomber . . . 123

Chapter 5: Engines 124

HISTORY

The Polish Aviation Museum in Cracow, established in 1963 is the only specialized aviation museum in Poland. It gathers and displays exhibits of world aviation technology and history and its collection is highly appreciated worldwide. The collection comprises airplanes, sailplanes, rotorcraft, aircraft engines, anti–aircraft missiles and radar. The Museum has also a library and archive with a vast collection of books and photographs.

The Museum occupies a part of the area of the former Cracow airfield Rakowice – Czyżyny, the oldest airfield in Poland and one of the oldest permanent airfields in Europe. As early as the turn of the 19th and 20th century the observation balloon company of the 2nd Fortress Artillery Regiment was based there. In 1912 the Austrian command established an aircraft maintenance unit, *Flugpark 7*, on the site. The aircraft from Rakowice took part in the defense of the Cracow fortress in 1914. In 1918 Rakowice became a stage airfield of the first regular airmail line, connecting Vienna with Kiev and Odessa. On October 31th, 1918 Polish military authorities assumed command of the base which became the first airfield of independent Poland. Also there the first Polish air unit, called the 1st Combat Squadron, was formed.

During the Polish – Soviet war the 1st Elementary Flying School for rapidly developing Polish military aviation was organized there. There were also aircraft maintenance workshops in which a limited production of new aircraft was undertaken. In 1921 the 2nd Air Regiment was formed basing on the existing technical infrastructure. In the late 1920s and 1930s Rakowice was the second largest military air base in Poland. In September 1939 the airfield was bombed and subsequently captured by the Germans, who subsequently developed it to the east towards the village of Czyżyny. In January 1945 the airfield was captured by the Soviets who handed it over to the Polish authorities six months later. The airfield was operated by the Air Force, Polish Airlines, medical transport and Cracow Aero Club. In 1963 the airfield was closed due to the development of the nearby steelworks and accompanying residential districts. Nowadays the airfield is again partially active as a landing site for helicopters and light aircraft. Cracow Police Helicopter Unit is based here. Since 2004

The Large Hangar, housing the main part of the exhibition

POLISH AVIATION MUSEUM CRACOW | 5

one of the greatest air displays in Poland, the Malopolska Air Show, has been organized on a 2,000 ft long remainder of concrete runway on the last weekend in June.

Many of the Museum's exhibits are unique specimens, like the fuselages of German combat aircraft from the First World War – the Halberstadt Cl.II, Albatros C.I, Aviatik C.III, DFW C.V oraz LFG Roland D.VIb, a complete Russian Grigorovich M-15 flying boat, German Albatros B.IIa trainer and the fuselages of the Albatros H.1 experimental aircraft and Sopwith F.1 Camel British fighter, one of five surviving.

The exhibits are displayed in three hangars, a new multi-function building and an open air exhibition. The main part of the exhibition is housed in the former hangar of the 2nd Air Regiment. The only surviving Polish pre-war PZL P.11c fighter, of the 121st Fighter Squadron/2nd Air Regiment, is displayed there. The other Polish pre-war aircraft are the PWS-26 trainer and RWD-13 and RWD-21 light sports aircraft. Among the Second World War aircraft the most notable are the British Supermarine Spitfire LF Mk XVI E fighter and Soviet Tupolev Tu-2S medium bomber, one of the best of its class at the end of hostilities. Next to the Tu-2 the only surviving Polikarpov Po-2 night bomber version is displayed. The exhibit documenting the resentful attitude of the Poles to the communist regime is the *Kukulka* (Cuckoo) amateur aircraft built by Eugeniusz Pieniazek, used by him to escape to Yugoslavia in 1971. The Museum also possesses airworthy Yakovlev Yak-18 and Piper Cub aircraft displayed at airshows by the pilots of the Polish Eagles foundation. Polish and foreign post-war aircraft, like TS-8 *Bies*, TS-9 *Junak*, Yak-18 and Aero L-200 *Morava*, operated by Polish military and civil aviation, are also displayed. Apart from them, a collection of Polish gliders built between the 1930s and 1990s can also be seen. The most interesting of them are the pre-war WWS *Wrona bis* and WWS-2 *Żaba* basic trainers, the only surviving SZD-43 *Orion* and the experimental, tailless SZD-6X *Nietoperz*, featuring a directional control system similar to the Northrop B-2 Spirit Stealth bomber.

The Museum possesses almost all types of combat jet aircraft ever operated by the Polish Air Force, among them a complete family of MiG-21s, gathered at an open air exhibition called "MiG Alley". That part of the collection is especially interesting for the visitors interested in Soviet combat aircraft of the Cold War era. They also may find the anti-aircraft S-125 *Newa*, SA-75 *Dźwina* and S-75M *Wołchow* rocket missiles interesting. Other noteworthy exhibits are the Ilyushin Il-14 and Yakovlev Yak-40 executive aircraft used by the leaders of communist Poland and later independent Poland.

There are also combat jets from the other side of the Iron Curtain. The SAAB J35J *Draken* fighter and SAAB AJSF37 *Viggen* reconnaissance aircraft represent the Air Force and industry of Sweden. The Northrop F-5E Tiger II and Cessna A-37B Dragonfly were operated by the Republic of Vietnam air force during the 1970s. The newest part of the collection is a group of aircraft operated by NATO member countries, gathered at the exhibition on the 60th anniversary of NATO, opened in 2009.

On the "You don't know your own... The stores of history" exhibition the relics of aircraft from various periods of aviation are displayed in original condition. A fuselage of the Messerschmitt Me-209V1 in which Fritz Wendel set the world speed record in 1939, or the Geest *Moewe* IV, AEG *Wagner Eule* and Levavasseur Antoinette aircraft, built before the First World War, are the most noteworthy.

A separate part of the collection is one of the world's largest aircraft engine exhibitions, in which engines from 1908 until the present are displayed. They include elements of the V-2 rocket missile propulsion system *Pegaz* II and *Pegaz* VIII radial engines, licence built in Poland, used in the PZL P.23 *Karaś* reconnaissance aircraft and *Pegaz* XX used in the PZL P.37 *Łoś* (Moose) bomber, and a BMW 801 radial engine, used in the German Focke-Wulf FW-190 fighter.

History

POLISH AVIATION MUSEUM CRACOW

The new building

The newest premise of the Polish Aviation Museum is a new, multi-function building, completed in 2010. The building has the shape of a three-bladed propeller and houses the exhibition hall, cinema, conference room, library and offices. As the building has the role of the entry gate to the museum, the exhibits displayed in a modern way are a kind of review of the whole Museum collection. Most of the exhibits were moved from other exhibitions, but some have not been displayed before. The new building is an element of a larger project for a theme park established on the former airfield, joining recreational, educational and cultural functions.

Aircraft for display in the new building:

Albatros B.IIa 10

TS-8 *Bies* 29

8 | POLISH AVIATION MUSEUM CRACOW

RWD-13 .... 22 RWD-21 .... 23 PWS-26 26

Bücker Bü - 131 *Jungmann* .... 50 *Kukułka* (Cuckoo) .... 30 JK-1 *Trzmiel* 53

IS-4 *Jastrząb* .... 60 SZD-6X *Nietoperz* .... 61 PZL TS-11 *Iskra* 92

POLISH AVIATION MUSEUM CRACOW | 9

Chapter 1: The Small Hangar

As we go through the wooden gates of the small hangar, we step back to the time of the First World War, which was a period of rapid development in aviation. Suddenly from the archaic pioneer constructions the aircraft became an efficient weapon.

The first military aircraft were used primarily for observation and reconnaissance. For these purposes the Albatros C.I, DFW C.V and Aviatik C.III, displayed at the Polish Aviation Museum, were designed. Later it was discovered that the aircraft might be used for fighting the enemy, and it was the task of the Halberstadt Cl.II, LFG Roland D.VIb or the famous British Sopwith F.1 Camel. Escalating air war required mass pilot training, performed on aircraft like the Albatros B.IIa and LVG B.II. Maritime operations caused the need to merge two elements and the Grigorovich M-15 flying boat is a successful example of such a machine. The exhibit closing

the collection is the Albatros H.1, a failed experimental modification of the Siemens-Schuckert D.IV fighter, built for test flights at high altitudes. But should the whole of First World War aviation not be considered as an experiment?

This part of the exhibition is a priceless treasure of the aviation museum collection. Except for the Sopwith Camel, all the aircraft are unique. They are the exhibits of the German Aircraft Collection, called Göring's Collection, which were evacuated from Berlin to Czarnkow in western Poland to avoid Allied bomber raids and in 1963 were placed at the Polish Aviation Museum in Cracow. All the aircraft were severely damaged. During the 1990s they were restored at the Museum's restoration facilities and placed on display. Most of them are incomplete – they lack wings, which were destroyed during the evacuation from Berlin.

Albatros B.IIa

Among the countless types of aircraft which appeared during the First World War there was no other which remained longer in production and was more versatile than the Albatros B.II. The German aviation press announced the existence of the Albatros DD (*Doppeldecker* - biplane) in 1913. Two variants, with two- and three-bay wing cellules, were developed. The three-bay version was later designated Albatros B.I, and the two-bay one the Albatros B.II. At the moment of its appearance, Albatros DD was a very modern design. Shortly before the outbreak of the First World War the Albatros biplanes showed their outstanding performance, breaking records for climb rate with full load, and also took part in the *Rallye de Monaco* and *Prinz Heinrich Flug* long distance flights. The Albatrosses were built in single and dual control versions. Aircraft in the dual control version were used in flying schools, and the single control ones, in which the pilot occupied the aft cockpit, served as reconnaissance aircraft on the front until mid 1915. They did not perform well in this role, because the observer, who occupied the front cockpit, had his view restricted by the lower wings. They did not carry armament, but later bomb racks and machine guns for defence against fighters were added as field modifications. From mid 1915 the Albatros C.I appeared, designed from the scratch as a reconnaissance and bomber aircraft, with the pilot occupying the front cockpit and a machine gun on a rotating turret in the aft cockpit, occupied by the observer. The shortage of steel, which began to affect Germany in the middle of the war resulted in the development of the B.IIa version, in which steel fuselage truss and landing gear struts were replaced by wooden elements. The production of this version commenced in 1917, as a supplement to the basic version.

Albatros B.IIa production was continued after the end of the war. Twenty aircraft were built, under the designation L30. Many aircraft of the type were left by the Germans on Polish territory after the end of hostilities. Those aircraft flew in independent Poland until the mid '30s, used primarily for pilot and observer training. The displayed aircraft is an Albatros B.IIa L30, built in 1919. Initially it had the German civil registration D-690, but later carried the military mark NG+UR, while being operated by the NSFK paramilitary organization. It was airworthy until May 25th, 1940, then it was handed over to the German Aircraft Collection. After the war it was severely damaged. In 1986 it underwent a thorough restoration at the Museum of Technology and Communication in West Berlin and since 1987 it has been on display in Cracow. It carries the paint scheme of Albatros B.IIa nr 1302/15 Ada, operated by the Officer Observer School at Torun in 1920. On the fuselage side a portrait of Ada Sari, a famous Polish pre-war operatic singer and actress, is painted.

12 | POLISH AVIATION MUSEUM CRACOW

DFW C.V

The prototype of the DFW C.V, which had the factory designation Type 29and was designed by Willi Sabersky-Müssigbrodt, first flew in the spring of 1916. It had outstanding flying characteristics. The first aircraft were assigned to combat units in October 1916 and immediately gained the respect of the crews thanks to good performance, easy handling and a spacious observer cockpit, with plenty of room for armament and photographic equipment. In late October 1916 the German Air Force command placed an order for 1,000 aircraft. Apart from the DFW factory, licence production was undertaken by the LVG, Aviatik and Halberstadt factories. Further orders followed and the production totalled around 3,250 aircraft. From April 1917 till September 1918 the DFW C.V was the most popular German type of multi purpose aircraft on the Western Front. They were used for reconnaissance, bombing and artillery cooperation. They flew on the Eastern Front and in Palestine as well. They were feared by Allied pilots. After the end of hostilities numerous aircraft were passed over to the *Deutsche Luft Reederei* company, the predecessor of *Lufthansa*, where they were used for passenger transport. On 17th June, 1919 a crew of this company set a new altitude record of 9,620 m (31,560 ft). Many aircraft served in the air forces of various countries, like Turkey, Finland, Bulgaria and Poland, which with 63 aircraft in service was one of the largest operators of the type. DFW C.V was one of the first aircraft types operated by the air force of independent Poland. The DFWs flew in combat during the war against the Ukrainians and Soviet Russia during 1918 – 1920.

Only one incomplete fuselage of the DFW C.V has survived until today. Aircraft number 17077/17 was built in 1917 at the DFW factory. In June 1918 it underwent an overhaul at the Automobil & Aviatik AG plant. After the war it was handed over to the German aircraft collection. During 1998 – 1999 it was restored at the Polish Aviation Museum and since then has been on display.

LFG Roland D.VIb

The LFG Roland D.VIb was a rather unsuccessful fighter aircraft, designed near the end of the First World War at the *Luftfahrzeuggesellschaft* (LFG) company in Berlin. It was a rival to the best German fighters of late World War I, the Fokker D.VII and Pfalz D.VIII, and was built as a supplement to the Fokker production. Its distinctive feature was the *Klinkerrumpf* – a fuselage of oval cross section, covered with strips of wood, resembling the hull of a clinker-built boat. The aircraft had good flying characteristics, but poor performance, due to an underpowered engine. 353 examples of the D.VIa and D.VIb versions were built, but they did not see any combat.

The Museum aircraft, number 2225/18, was flown by Hermann Göring during the Second Fighter Competition at Adlershof (1st June – 15th July, 1918).

14 | POLISH AVIATION MUSEUM CRACOW

ALBATROS C.I

The Albatros C.I was the first German C-class aircraft – armed, two seat biplane, used for reconnaissance and bombing. It was the first aircraft to feature the patent of Franz Schneider – a machine gun mounted on a rotating turret in the aft cockpit, enabling the protection of the aircraft's rear hemisphere. The Albatros C.I was based on the Albatros B.II design, and from mid 1915 on began to replace the latter type in combat units.

The displayed aircraft, number 197/15, was operated during 1917 – 1918 by the Officer Wireless Operators School at Mokotów airfield in Warsaw, then occupied by the Germans. Later it belonged to the German Aircraft Collection. In 1993 it underwent a thorough restoration at the Polish Aviation Museum's workshop and since then has been on display.

Albatros H.1

The Albatros H.1 was an unsuccessful experimental aircraft, built in the mid '20s, intended for test flights at high altitudes of about 30,000 ft. It was a modification of the World War I Siemens-Schuckert D.IV fighter. The modifications included wings of increased span and propeller of increased diameter to enable flying in thin air at high altitudes. As the new wings proved to be too weak, in this shape the aircraft did not make a single flight and was handed over to the German Aircraft Collection. The Albatros H.1 was powered by Siemens-Halske Sh-III birotary engine, in which the cylinders and crankcase with the propeller rotated in one direction, and the crankshaft in the opposite direction. Unlike other rotary engines, this one had full throttle control.

16 | POLISH AVIATION MUSEUM CRACOW

Aviatik C.III

The Aviatik C.III was a two seat reconnaissance and bomber aircraft, designed and built by Automobil und Aviatik AG company in Mühlhausen (Mulhouse), Alsace. Production ran during 1916 – 1917. It was not a very successful design, and the Aviatik company ceased its production after having built about 80, and undertook the licence production of the DFW C.V, a far better airplane. The fuselage is covered with fabric, which was more characteristic for British and French than German aircraft.

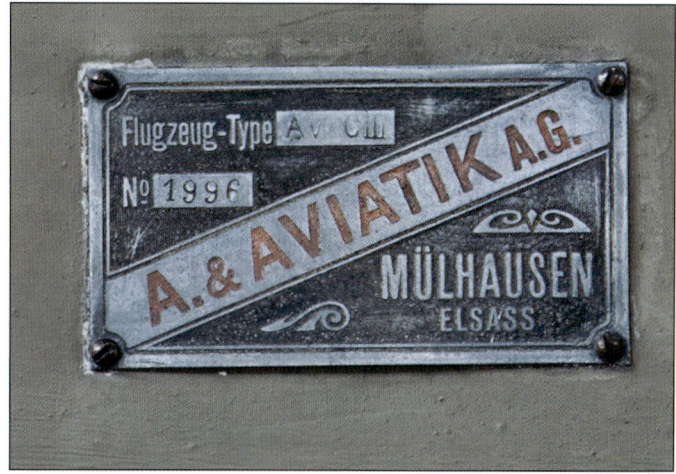

LVG B.II

In 1912 Franz Schneider, a Swiss engineer previously with Nieuport, joined Luft-Verkehrs GmbH located at Berlin – Johannisthal, and designed a tractor biplane, the LVG B.I, which made its first flight in 1913. This type of construction was given the name the Schneider system. In German nomenclature the letter B indicated unarmed two-seat biplanes. The B.II was very similar to the B.I, but had some small modifications in order to achieve better operational performance. It became the main production model and from 1915 was widely used as a training and light reconnaissance aircraft. The LVG B.II had very good flight and safety characteristics, thus it performed well its role as a trainer and was liked by pilots.

The displayed aircraft, serial number 350/17, built in 1917 by Luftfahrzeugbau Schutte – Lanz, is the only one to survive.

18 | POLISH AVIATION MUSEUM CRACOW

Halberstadt Cl.II

Designing the Halberstadt Cl.II as an escort fighter for protection of reconnaissance airplanes, nobody expected that this type would become the first attack aircraft. On 6th September, 1917 twenty-four Halberstadts massacred British cavalry troops crossing the Somme river. Their combat records meant that they were perceived as invincible, armoured airplanes, which was inaccurate because the aircraft had mediocre flying characteristics, an underpowered engine and high vulnerability. A number of these aircraft saw service with the air force of reborn Poland, taking part in the war against Soviet Russia.

The displayed fuselage is of Halberstadt Cl.II, number 15459/17, the personal aircraft of Lt Gen. Ernst von Höppner, one of the commanders of the German Air Force during the First World War.

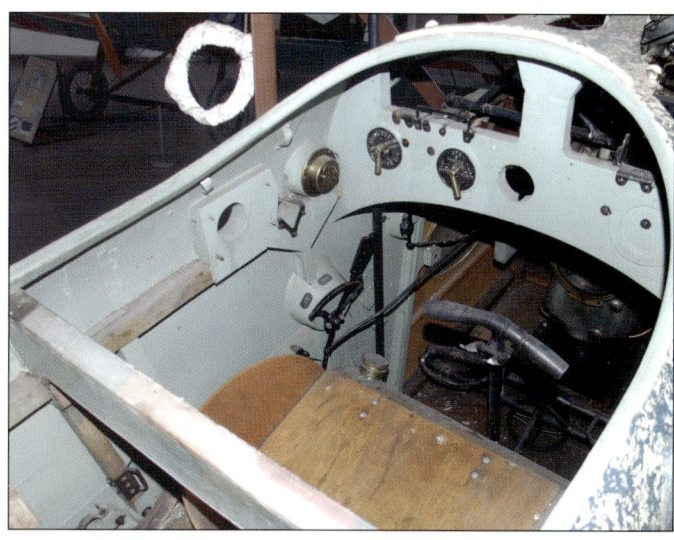

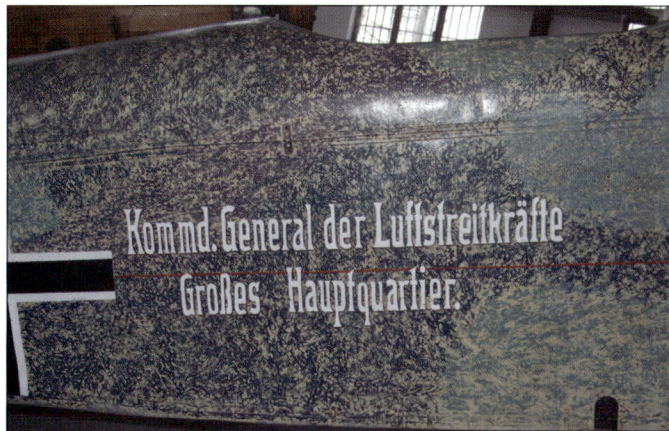

Sopwith F.1 Camel

The Sopwith F.1 Camel was a single-seat fighter biplane, designed during late 1916 by Thomas Sopwith as a successor to the Sopwith Pup fighter. It became the most famous British aircraft of World War One. First Camels entered service in Royal Navy Air Service (RNAS) squadrons in May and in Royal Flying Corps (RFC) squadrons in July 1917. Several versions were built, powered by various types of engines and differing in performance. The total production was 5490 aircraft.

The Sopwith Camel was famous for its superb agility, but the torque generated by the rotary engine made it very difficult to fly, especially for inexperienced pilots, and as a result it was the first fighter of which a two seat training version was developed. The Camel was also the first single-seat fighter which could carry bombs.

The displayed aircraft, serial number B 7280, was built at the Clayton & Shuttleworth factory in Lincoln. On 30th March, 1918 it was assigned to 1 RNAS squadron (renamed 201 Royal Air Force Squadron on 1th April, 1918). Flying Officer J. H. Foreman destroyed two German aircraft flying this plane. After an overhaul, this aircraft was assigned to 210 RAF Squadron and was flown by Flight Lieutenant H.A. Patey DFC, who scored nine victories between 16th June and 5th September, 1918. On 5th September he force landed behind German lines and the aircraft was captured by the Germans. After flight tests it was transferred to the German Aircraft Collection. It is one of five aircraft of the type remaining. It is fitted with a bomb rack, the only genuine one surviving.

20 | POLISH AVIATION MUSEUM CRACOW

Grigorovich M-15

The Grigorovich M-15 was a reconnaissance flying boat, designed by Dmitrii Grigorovich at the Shcherbakov & Shchetinin factory in St. Petersburg in 1917. The M-15, based on the model M-9, was ordered by the Imperial Russian Navy in 1915. The powerplant was a French Hispano-Suiza V-8 engine. The development timeline of this aircraft covers three époques in history of Russia in a short time. Designed under the reign of the Tsar, built during the period after the February Revolution, when Russia was a republic (March – November 1917) and withdrawn from production after the outbreak of the October Revolution due to engine supply problems. Eighty Grigorovich M-15s were built.

The displayed aircraft, serial number R II C 262, was delivered to the air squadron of the Arensburg fortress on the Isle of Saarema (Gulf of Riga). It was captured by the Germans during Operation Albion (10th – 24th October 1917) and sent for tests at the German Naval Research Center at Warnemünde, later transferred to the German Aircraft Collection. The aircraft was restored at the Museum during 1991 – 1993. The engine was brought back to working condition.

Chapter 2: 1930s to the Present

The main part of the exhibition, military and civil aircraft from the inter-war period, Second World War and post-war years, is housed in the historical hangar of the 2nd Air Regiment.

The hangar itself is a very interesting monument of aerodrome architecture. It was completed in 1930 and was used by the technical department of the 2nd Air Regiment. Professor Izydor Stella-Sawicki and Engineer S. Koziolek designed the steel bearer construction, with the roof suspended under the arches, which became standard in Polish aerodrome architecture. There were six such hangars at Cracow airfield. They were destroyed by the Germans, retreating before the advancing Red Army in January 1945. The Museum's hangar and Polish Airlines hangar, today situated outside the area of the Museum, were rebuilt in the early 1950s.

The most noteworthy exhibits are Second World War fighters – the PZL P.11c and Supermarine Spitfire LF Mk XVIe, bombers and attack aircraft – Tu-2S, Po-2 LNB and Avia B-33 (Czech licence-built Ilyushin Il-10, the successor of the Il-2 *Shturmovik*) and observation Piper L-4A Grasshopper, operated

by the US Army in Northern Africa during 1943 – 1945, then purchased by Poland from American surplus. Many aircraft gathered here were used for the pilot training during the Second World War, like the Polish PWS-26, German Bücker Bü-131 *Jungmann*, British de Havilland Tiger Moth and American North American T-6G Texan and Cessna UC-78A Bobcat. Other rarities are the only surviving RWD sports aircraft in Poland – the RWD-13 and RWD-21, belonging to the family of light aircraft built in Poland during the late 1920s and 1930s. Aircraft from this family contributed to three greatest pre-war successes of Polish sport aviation – victories in the Challenge competitions in 1932 (crew Franciszek Żwirko and Stanislaw Wigura in an RWD-6) and 1934 (crew Jerzy Bajan and Gustaw Pokrzywka in an RWD-9) and the first transatlantic flight by a Polish pilot, Stanislaw Skarżyński in an RWD-5*bis* in 1933.

There are also exhibits documenting the development of two new families of aircraft, which appeared in Poland after the Second World War – jets and rotorcraft. To the right side from the entrance the two first jets operated by the Polish Air Force are displayed – the Yakovlev Yak 17W trainer and Yak-23 fighter. The rotorcraft collection comprises experimental helicopters SP-GIL and JK-1 *Trzmiel* and series production SM-1, SM-2 and Mi-2 in the URP attack version.

Under the roof are suspended numerous sailplanes, documenting 60 years of Polish gliding. Among them are WWS *Wrona* (Crow) and *Żaba* (Frog), IS-C *Żuraw* (Crane), SZD-10 *Czapla* trainers, competition SZD-8 and SZD-17X *Jaskółka* (Swallow), SZD-19 *Zefir* (Zephyr), aerobatic IS-4 *Jastrząb* (Hawk), SZD-21 *Kobuz* and Swift S-1, and experimental SZD-6X *Nietoperz* (Bat).

RWD-13

The RWD-13 is a three-seater tourist aircraft, designed to the order of the LOPP (League for Air and Gas Defense) by Stanisław Rogalski, Jerzy Drzewiecki and Leszek Dulęba at DWL (Experimental Aviation Works) at Okęcie airfield in Warsaw. The design of the RWD-13 originated from the RWD-6 and RWD-9, which won the International Tourist Aircraft Contests (Challenge) in 1932 and 1934. RWD-13 is a highwing aircraft of mixed construction. The fuselage is a welded steel tube truss covered with fabric. The wings were of strut-braced design, with a wooden structure covered with plywood and fabric, and fitted with Handley-Page slats. The powerplant was either a PZInż Major or DH Gipsy Major engine, rated at 130 hp. The aircraft has short take off and landing characteristics (STOL) and features backward folding wings for easy storage. The prototype first flew on January 15th, 1935 and after flying tests entered production. In 1937 ambulance, and in 1938 ambulance/tourer, versions were developed. Production totalled 83 aircraft of all versions between 1935 and 1939.

RWD-13 were operated by aero clubs, LOPP flying schools, Ministry of Transport, Polish Airlines LOT, private companies like Polish Philips Works or E. Wedel Chocolate Factory and individuals. Military aviation operated aircraft in the ambulance version. Some RWD-13s were sold abroad – to the USA, Brazil, Spain, Palestine, Yemen and Iran. In 1938 the Yugoslav Rogozarski Aircraft Factory built six aircraft under licence. The RWD-13 exported to Spain served with General Franco's Nationalist forces during the Civil War, and the ones sold to Palestine flew in combat during the Israel Liberation War during 1947 – 1948.

After the outbreak of World War II several RWD-13s performed liaison duties. A number of aircraft were evacuated to Romania, Estonia and Sweden. The aircraft evacuated to Romania were used by the Romanian Air Force for liaison and medical transport duties during the hostilities with the USSR and then Germany. After the war, two RWD-13s were brought back to Poland. One of them, with the registration SP-BNU, belongs to the Polish Aviation Museum in Cracow. There is also an airworthy RWD-13 with the registration PT-LFY in Brazil.

24 | POLISH AVIATION MUSEUM CRACOW

RWD-21

The RWD-21 was designed by Andrzej Anczutin during 1938 – 1939 at the Experimental Aviation Works in Warsaw as a simple, cheap and economical trainer and tourer of wooden construction. It was a further development of the RWD-16*bis*, with a more powerful engine. The prototype, displayed now at the Museum, made its first flight in February 1939 with Eugeniusz Przysiecki at the controls. The aircraft proved to be a successful design and series production was undertaken. Five aircraft for private owners were built.

After the outbreak of the war two aircraft – SP-BRH and the prototype SP-BPE - were evacuated to Romania. Both were subsequently ferried from Mlociny airfield in Warsaw to Świdnik by Bronislaw Żurakowski, who was then a glider pilot, in order to rescue precious aircraft. He was flying the airplane for the first time, which is a good testimony of RWD-21's flying characteristics. In Romania SP-BPE was operated with registration YR-VEN. In 1947 it was flown back to Poland and until the mid 1950s flew as SP-AKG.

PZL P.11c

The PZL P.11c is one of the most famous and valuable exhibits of the Polish Aviation Museum. Aircraft number 8.63 is the only surviving example of the type. This airplane is a monument to the achievements of the Polish aviation industry of the inter-war period and symbol of the heroic struggle of Polish pilots against the predominant forces of Nazi Germany in September 1939.

The PZL P.11c is one of the most important designs in the history of Polish aviation. It was the type of fighter aircraft produced in greatest number before the war in Poland, with 175 built. It belongs to the family of all metal high-wing fighters, of which the first one was the PZL P.1, designed by Zygmunt Puławski in 1928. The aircraft featured some outstanding design features developed by Puławski – the so-called gull wing, tapering at the root, and landing gear with shock struts hidden within the fuselage, which were exceptionally advanced in the early 1930s. In 1934 at the Le Bourget Air Fair the aircraft was declared the most modern fighter in the world. A licence for P.11 production was purchased by the Romanian IAR company.

At the outbreak of the Second World War the P.11c was the mainstay of the Polish fighter force and was the main type to fight the *Luftwaffe*, which had great superiority in numbers and quality. Despite this vast disproportion the Polish pilots flying the P.11c managed to shoot down about 130 German aircraft. Most P.11s were destroyed, some

were evacuated to Romania and Hungary where they served until the end of the war.

The displayed P.11c, number 8-63, belonged to the 122nd Fighter Squadron of the 2nd Air Regiment based at Cracow. It was assigned to 2nd Lt Wacław Krol. After the end of the Defensive War in 1939 it was captured by the Germans and sent to the German Aircraft Collection and with the other exhibits of the collection was evacuated to western Poland and abandoned there. As the only surviving example of the type it is one of the most valuable monuments of air and military technology in Poland. The aircraft is complete, with its engine in working condition.

PWS-26

The PWS-26 is a two-seat trainer, designed in 1935 as the last of the family of PWS military trainers, started by the PWS-12. It is a biplane of mixed construction, adapted for inverted flights as well as bombing and gunnery training. The armament comprised a 7.7 mm (0.303 in) Vickers wz. 33 machine gun, two 12 kg (25 lb) bombs and a gun camera. The powerplant was a 240 hp Skoda-Wright J5 Whirlwind radial engine. The top speed was 200 km/h. It was the second most-produced aircraft, after the RWD-8, in Poland before the Second World War, with 260 built.

After the outbreak of war some PWS-26s were evacuated to Latvia and Romania. The Germans captured 30 and overhauled them at Mielec. Two aircraft were tested in Germany, the others were sold to Romania. Many aircraft were captured and operated by the Soviets.

The displayed aircraft, number 81-123, was built in 1937 and is the only survivor. In 1939 it was captured by the Germans and displayed at the German Aircraft Collection. In 1943 with other exhibits of the collection it was evacuated to western Poland and thus survived the war. During 1949-1953 it was operated by Polish aero clubs with the registration SP-AJB. In 1951 it was used as a tow plane during the trials of the SZD-6X *Nietoperz* (Bat) glider. In the 1960s was handed over to the Polish Aviation Museum. In 1996 it underwent restoration at the Museum's restoration facility.

POLISH AVIATION MUSEUM CRACOW

Curtiss Hawk II

In 1923 the American Curtiss Aeroplane & Motor Corporation commenced production of mixed construction Hawk fighters in land and maritime versions. In 1932 the F-11C Goshawk with radial engine was developed, which entered service as carrier-based fighter and dive bomber. A simplified export version, designated Hawk II, was sold to China, Thailand, Turkey and many South American countries.

During his visit to the USA one of the most famous German aviators, Ernst Udet, was amazed by a display of dive bombing by the Hawks and decided that this aircraft would be the basis of studies on future German dive bombers. As the Treaty of Versailles forbade Germany to maintain an air force, two unarmed Hawks with civil registrations D-IRIS and D-IRIK were purchased. The former crashed on 20th July, 1934 and Ernst Udet, who was piloting it, managed to bail out. The latter, of which the fuselage is now displayed at the Polish Aviation Museum, took part in various air shows during 1934-1937, including the Olympic Games in Berlin in 1936, and then belonged to the German Aircraft Collection. It is unique.

TS-9 Junak 3

The TS-9 *Junak* 3 is a two seat low wing aircraft of mixed construction with tricycle landing gear, designed in 1952 by Tadeusz Sołtyk, used for pilot training in the Air Force and aero clubs. It is a further development version of the LWD *Junak* 2 with a tailwheel. Between 1954 and 1956 146 aircraft were built by WSK PZL Okęcie at Warsaw. The *Junak* 3s entered service in the Air Force, where they were operated until 1961 and were replaced by the TS-8 *Bies*. The aircraft were retired from the Air Force to the aero clubs. The last one, registered SP-BOG, was written off in 1972.

The displayed aircraft, serial number 13-9578, was built in 1955 within the last production batch. Initially it was operated by the Officer Flying School at Dęblin and then, with the registration SP-BPL, by the Cracow Aero Club, who donated it to the Museum in 1969.

30 | POLISH AVIATION MUSEUM CRACOW

TS-8 *Bies*

The TS-8 *Bies* (Devil) is a two-seat trainer, designed by Tadeusz Sołtyk, powered by a WN-3 radial engine, earmarked mainly for military aviation. It was the first all-metal aircraft designed and built in Poland after the Second World War. It had very good flight characteristics. 229 aircraft were built during 1957-1960. In 1966 the first *Bies* aircraft, retired from the Air Force, were handed over to aero clubs, where they operated until 1978. Indonesia purchased two aircraft, adapted for a tropical climate. The *Bies* broke three world records in its class – altitude record of 7,084 m (23,241 ft), and a year later set a closed-circuit distance record of 2,884 km (1,557 NM) and speed in a 2,000 km (1,080 NM) long closed circuit of 320 km/h (173 kt).

The Museum possesses two aircraft of the type – the prototype and a series production TS-8 BII *Bies*, number 0309, built in 1958 and donated by the Polish Air Force Command in 1967.

Kukułka (Cuckoo)

Eugeniusz Pieniążek is an amateur designer. During the late 1960s, when he was working at the Gliding Center in Leszno, he demonstrated Polish gliders in Sweden and he made friends with Swedish airmen. Because of this he was repressed by the Security Service (communist political police) after his return, which led him to the decision to leave Poland. He had no chance to get a passport and leave legally, neither did he want to steal an aircraft from an aero club, so he decided to build his own aircraft which would fly him to freedom.

The general design was based on the British single-seat Turbulent amateur airplane. In the construction process parts from different aircraft were utilized – shortened wings and canopy from a crashed SZD-8 *Jaskółka* (Swallow) glider, tailplane from a SZD-24 *Foka* (Seal) glider, control stick from a *Zefir* glider and a Continental A-65 engine and landing gear from a Piper Cub. The main part of the construction process took place in Pieniążek's apartment in a block of flats in Leszno, in his daughter's room with an area of 8 square meters. Completed elements, which were too large to be carried down the stairway, were lowered down from the window on ropes. The final assembly took place at Leszno airfield. The name "Cuckoo" was suggested by Pieniążek's seven year old daughter, Izabela. The *Kukułka* first flew in spring of 1971 and as the first amateur aircraft in the People's Republic of Poland was officially registered as SP-PHN. During the summer of 1971 Pieniążek was flying the *Kukułka* around Poland and trained 44 other pilots on the aircraft.

On the morning of 13th September 1971 Eugeniusz Pieniążek flew the from Bielsko-Biała to Krosno in south–eastern Poland. He was expected to be back the same afternoon. After take off from Krosno he turned south and after a three-hour low level flight over Czechoslovakia and Hungary, in a severe rainstorm, with the engine on the brink of seizing due to low oil pressure, he landed at Subotica, Yugoslavia. In Poland he was declared missing, probably dead. He spent seven months in Yugoslav prisons and then he was allowed to go through the "green border" to Austria, from where in May 1972 he emigrated to Sweden. In 1973 Mr and Mrs Pieniążek drove a Volkswagen Beetle to Subotica to collect the *Kukułka* and take it to Sweden. He towed the fuselage and the wings were laid on top of the car.

After arrival in Sweden the *Kukułka* spent 17 years in a hangar at Eskilstuna. In 1990 it was brought back to airworthy status. A new engine and landing gear were necessary. A more powerful Continental A-90 and landing gear with fiberglass struts were mounted. The *Kukułka* flew for three years in Sweden. In 1993 Pieniążek brought it to Poland. In 1996 the *Kukułka* was again registered, as SP-FKU, but later the original markings SP-PHN were reinstated. In 2005 television made a documentary series "The Great Escapes". One episode was about the escape of Pieniążek in the *Kukułka*.

On 13th September 2005 Eugeniusz Pieniążek donated the *Kukułka* to the Polish Aviation Museum.

Piper L-4A Grasshopper

The Piper Cub was developed in the 1930s in the USA as a light trainer. In 1941 it won the US Army competition for a light liaison and artillery target spotting aircraft. The military designation was O-59, later changed to L-4 Grasshopper. The combat debut took place during the "Operation Torch" US landings in North Africa. During the war the L-4 was used in great numbers on all fronts. The aircraft had no standard armament, but in many units they were retrofitted with infantry armament, for example Bazooka antitank missile launchers. The Cub stood out for its simplicity of construction and flying. 5,500 aircraft were built in several versions, ranging from the L-4A to the L-4J.

After the war Poland purchased from American surplus 141 aircraft, of which 127 were registered. They were operated by aero clubs and agricultural aviation. In early 1950s most of them were scrapped, because they were "politically incorrect" as "imperialistic aircraft".

Many Piper Cubs still fly throughout the world, including Poland. The aircraft SP-AFY, built in 1944, is the oldest aircraft registered in Poland. With short breaks for overhauls it has been in service since 1947. The Piper Cub design was the base for several similar constructions.

The displayed aircraft, serial number 43-29233, was built in 1943. It served with the 9th US Army in North Africa and Italy. After the war it was purchased by Poland and registered SP-AFP. It was used as an executive aircraft of the Experimental Aviation Works at Łódź and then in the Świdnik Aero Club, which donated it to the Museum in 1976.

POLISH AVIATION MUSEUM CRACOW | 33

North American T-6G Texan

North American T-6G Texan is an all-metal low wing aircraft with retractable landing gear, powered by a 600-hp radial engine, used for advanced training of military pilots, developed in the USA in 1937. The BC-1 version for the US Army Air Corps and the SNJ version for the US Navy were developed. After the change of the designation system in the USAAC the BC-1 was redesignated AT-6 Texan. It was produced and used during the Second World War. The British version, differing from the American version by the cockpit equipment, was designated Harvard. Polish pilots also were also trained on these aircraft in Great Britain and Canada. Texans (or derivatives of the design) were licence-built in Australia, Canada and Sweden. In total, more than 20,000 aircraft were built.

After the end of the war the Texans were being phased out, but the lack of new aircraft forced a rethink. In 1949 the production plants started to collect all the existing AT-6 aircraft. After a thorough examination of all components, new aircraft, designated T-6G, were assembled from the most valuable components. In this way, 2,600 aircraft were assembled in the USA and Canada.

Between 1945 and 1959 the Texans were exported to more than 50 countries. Apart from pilot training, they were used as light attack aircraft in several local conflicts, e.g. in Algeria and Congo. Nowadays the Texan is one of the most popular warbirds, many aircraft around the world still fly. Texans starred in several war films, including acting as Japanese Mitsubishi A6M Zero fighters.

The displayed aircraft, serial number 49-2983, was built in 1949. Between 1954 and 1961 it flew combat missions with the French Air Force in Algeria.

Cessna UC-78A Bobcat

In 1939 the Cessna Aircraft Corporation developed its first twin engine aircraft, the five seat, mixed construction low wing Cessna T-50, designed by Tom Selter. It was powered by two 245 hp Jacobs radial engines. In 1940 the military became interested, and mass production began. Under the designation AT-8/AT-17 Bobcats served as multi engine trainers, as UC-78 (utility/cargo) for liaison and transport duties. 2,042 aircraft of all versions were built.

After the war Poland purchased 21 Bobcats from American surplus, of which 14 were registered and the rest were a source of spare parts. They were used by Polish Airlines LOT for pilot training and executive flights. In the early 1950s all but one aircraft were scrapped. The only survivor, now displayed in the Museum, was handed over to the Aviation Institute, where it was used as an executive aircraft between 1952 and 1967 with the registration SP-GLC. In July 1953 record-setting parachute jumps from 4,600 and 4,800 meters were made from it.

The sharkmouth painted on the nose commemorates the fact that SP-GLC owes its long life to the cannibalization of other aircraft of the type.

POLISH AVIATION MUSEUM CRACOW | 35

De Havilland DH-82A Tiger Moth

DH.82 Tiger Moth is a trainer biplane designed by Geoffrey de Havilland as a development version of the earlier DH.60T Moth Trainer. The prototype first flew on 26th October 1931. The aircraft was powered by 120 hp Gipsy Major inverted inline engine. The upper wing was moved forward to make baling out from the front cockpit easier, and a slight sweep was applied to the wings to counter the center of gravity relocation. The Tiger Moth aroused RAF interest and entered service as a trainer in 1932. 114 aircraft were built by de Havilland, 3 in Sweden and 17 in Norway. In 1937 the most popular version, the DH.82A powered by a 130 hp engine, was developed. Mass production commenced after the outbreak of the Second World War, when the need for pilots increased rapidly. 2,889 aircraft were built by de Havilland and 2,572 by Morris Motors in Great Britain, licence production was undertaken in Canada (de Havilland Canada – 30); Australia (de Havilland Aircraft Pty - 1,070) and New Zealand (de Havilland Aircraft of New Zealand – 133). 91 aircraft were also built in Portugal and 20 in Norway and Sweden. After the war many surplus aircraft were sold to private owners. Many were used in agriculture, mainly in Australia and Great Britain. Today the Tiger Moth is one of the most popular old aircraft – about 200 aircraft are still airworthy.

Tiger Moths were also use by Polish flying schools in Great Britain during the Second World War. The displayed aircraft sports the paint scheme of aircraft number T-8209, operated by the Polish 25th Elementary Flying Training School at Hucknall in 1943.

36 | POLISH AVIATION MUSEUM CRACOW

Supermarine Spitfire LF Mk XVIe

The Supermarine Spitfire is an aircraft legend, familiar even to people not interested in aviation. As the main type of fighter in the RAF it is one of the warplanes which contributed the most to the Allied victory in the Second World War.

The Spitfire was designed by Reginald Mitchell, basing on his experience in designing racing floatplanes, which in the 1920s were winning the Schneider Trophy – a prestigious award for high speed flight. The Royal Air Force in 1933 ordered a new fighter aircraft from Vickers Supermarine. The prototype of Supermarine Type 300, later named Spitfire, with RAF serial K5054, made its first flight on March 5th, 1936. It was a metal low wing aircraft, powered by a Rolls-Royce Merlin V-12 engine, with retractable landing gear and enclosed cockpit, with characteristic elliptical wings housing eight 7.7 mm (0.303in) Vickers machine guns. In 1938 the Mk I entered production. During the Battle of Britain in 1940 Spitfires comprised about one third of RAF Fighter Command, but with the progress of the war it became the main type of fighter aircraft. Subsequent variants were powered by more powerful engines and with different armament. The advent of a new German fighter – the Focke-Wulf Fw-190 in 1942 - caused a rapid increase in British losses, which forced the development of a variant which could meet the Focke-Wulf on equal terms. A new Rolls-Royce Merlin 61, optimized for high altitudes and with a more efficient cooling system was mounted in the Mk V airframe, and so the Mk IX variant was created. It became the most numerous Spitfire variant, in service from mid 1942 until 1945.

This airplane is closely connected with the history of the struggle of Polish airmen against the *Luftwaffe*. All Polish fighter squadrons in Great Britain operated this type during 1943-1944, and some of them, like 302, 308 and 317 Squadrons, operated Spitfire Mk IXs until the end of the war.

The Mk XVI was a derivation of the Mk IX, powered by American licence-built Packard Merlin 266 engine.

The displayed aircraft is an LF Mk XVIe variant, optimised for low altitude. The aircraft had RAF serial number SM 411. It was assigned to 421 RCAF Squadron, with code letters AU-Y.

POLISH AVIATION MUSEUM CRACOW | 37

In 1968 it took part in the making of "The Battle of Britain" movie. In 1977 it was exchanged with the Polish Aviation Museum for a DH-9A, now displayed at the RAF Museum in Hendon. The aircraft is not complete – it lacks a gyroscopic gunsight, which was removed by the British before sending the aircraft to Poland, as it was still considered a classified device, which should not be sent to a communist country. In Poland the Spitfire was displayed in 421 Squadron markings, then it obtained the colors of TB 866, ZF-O, flown by F/O Henryk Krakowian of Polish 308 Squadron, based at Gilze-Rijen, Netherlands, in April 1945.

38 | POLISH AVIATION MUSEUM CRACOW

Polikarpov Po-2 LNB

The Polikarpov U-2, later renamed Po-2, was designed by N. Polikarpov in 1928 as a basic trainer. It is a wooden biplane of very simple construction adapted for operations in most primitive conditions by unqualified personnel with poor technical background. After the outbreak of the Second World War this already archaic airplane was adapted to the night bomber role and performed quite well. The aircraft could approach the target in a shallow dive unnoticed, with engine running quietly at idle, drop bombs and escape before AA guns opened fire. Units operating this type frequently consisted of women, called "Night Witches" by the Germans. The Po-2s were also flown by Poles. One of the aviation units established in the USSR within the Polish People's Army was the 2nd Night Bomber Regiment Cracow. The displayed aircraft, serial number 641-646, White 4, belonged to that unit. It is the only remaining example of the Po-2 bomber version.

POLISH AVIATION MUSEUM CRACOW | 39

Tupolev Tu-2S

The Tu-2 is a medium bomber, designed by a team supervised by Andrei Tupolev during the early 1940s. In the history of aviation it became famous as an aircraft designed in prison, because by the order of Stalin the whole of Tupolev's team had been imprisoned at Lubianka, where it received orders to design a fast dive bomber. After the outbreak of the war priorities changed and Tupolev was tasked to design a fast frontline horizontal bomber. This design, accepted in March 1940, was designated 103. The prototype, with inline engines, first flew in January 1941. The next prototype 103W, powered by radial engines, became the pattern for series production. In May 1942 it was designated Tu-2 and in the same year it entered combat service. In 1943 an upgraded version Tu-2S, with new ASh-82FN engines, was developed, which entered mass production in 1944 and 2,527 aircraft were built by 1947.

After the Second World War the Tu-2S was the main type of Soviet light bomber until the Il-28 entered service. Tu-2S also saw combat during the Korean War. In Poland seven aircraft were operated by the Air Force and Naval Aviation during 1950-1957. At the end of their service they were used as target tugs. The displayed aircraft ended its service as a flying testbed for ejection seats, which were mounted in the upper gunner's position.

Yakovlev Yak-11

The Yak-11 was developed in 1946 in the USSR at the Yakovlev design bureau as an advanced trainer, a type between the Po-2 and UT-2 basic trainers and fighter aircraft. The Yak-11 was based on the Yak-3 fighter design. The powerplant was the 700 hp ASh-21 radial engine. Series production began in 1947 and at the end of that year the first aircraft entered service. 3,859 aircraft were built. They were exported to many countries, including Poland, Austria, Albania, Algeria, Afghanistan, Bulgaria, China, Egypt, Yemen, Iraq, Guinea and East Germany. They were also licence-built in Czechoslovakia. The aircraft had good flight characteristics, but was difficult to fly due to the great torque generated by the propeller.

In Poland the first Yak-11s appeared in 1949. They were used in the Officer Flying Schools at Radom and Dęblin and as trainers in fighter units. In 1953 the first Czech-built aircraft, designated Ch-11, arrived in Poland. The Yak-11s remained in service until 1962.

The displayed aircraft, serial number 64236, was built in the USSR. After being retired in 1962 it was sent to the Air Display on the 20th anniversary of the People's Republic of Poland in Cracow, which was the beginning of the Polish Aviation Museum collection.

Yakovlev Yak-12

The Yak-12 is a utility aircraft, designed in the USSR at the Yakovlev design bureau as the successor of the Po-2. The prototype first flew in 1947. It is a high wing aircraft of metal construction, with braced wings and fabric covered fuselage. The first version of the Yak-12, as possessed by the Museum, was powered by 160 hp M-11FR radial engine. In 1955 the Yak-12M version, powered by a 260 hp AI-14 engine, was developed. In 1957 a subsequent version, Yak-12A with redesigned wings and better performance, appeared.

The Yak-12M and Yak-12A aircraft were licence-built in large numbers by the WSK PZL Warszawa-Okęcie plant. They were used as liaison aircraft in the Air Force, by aero clubs and medical transport teams. Until the present they have been used in aero clubs as glider tugs and for dropping parachute jumpers.

The displayed aircraft, serial number 5013, was built in 1951. During 1951-1952 it served with the Air Force, then in civil aviation until 1973, registered SP-ASZ. In 1973 it was donated to the Museum by the WSK PZL Mielec.

42 | POLISH AVIATION MUSEUM CRACOW

Yakovlev Yak-18

The Yak-18 is a two-seat low wing trainer, the successor of the UT-2, designed in 1937 by A. Yakovlev, on which Polish pilots were trained in the USSR during the Second World War and after the war in Poland. The Yak-18 was designed in 1946 and series production commenced in 1947 and continued until 1957. 5,680 aircraft were built in the USSR and Hungary. The Yak-18U with tricycle landing gear, Yak-18A powered by the AI-14 engine, four seat Yak-18T and single seat aerobatic Yak-18P, PM and PS versions were also built. In 1975 the Yak-50 aerobatic aircraft, powered by the M-14 engine, and in 1978 the two seat Yak-52 trainer were developed. Both originated from the Yak-18 design.

In Poland the Yak-18s were operated between 1950 and 1978 by the Air Force and aero clubs.

The displayed aircraft, serial number 9732, was built in the USSR in 1955. Initially it was operated by the Officer Flying School at Dęblin and then, with the registration SP-BRI, by the Cracow Aero Club, which donated it to the Museum in 1972.

The Museum owns also the only airworthy Yak-18 in Poland, registered SP-YYY, built in Hungary in 1956. It is leased to the Polish Eagles Foundation in exchange for the Messerschmitt Bf 109.

Yakovlev Yak-17UTI

In 1946 the first jet fighter by Yakovlev made its first flight, the Yak-15 based on the piston powered Yak-3 design, with a step-type fuselage (with jet engine housed in nose part of the fuselage and characteristic ventral step behind the exhaust nozzle). A two-seat training version, named Yak-17UTI (also designated Yak-17W) with a tricycle landing gear was developed and entered production, together with the fighter version Yak-17. These aircraft were powered by RD-10 engines, a Soviet copy of the Junkers Jumo 004.

The Yak-17UTI was not a successful design. Its major drawbacks were short flight endurance due to small fuel capacity, low speed, poor equipment and inability to operate all major systems from the instructor's cockpit, which significantly restricted its training capabilities. A total of 430 aircraft was built. The Polish Air Force operated 6 aircraft between 1951 and 1955. They were assigned to Yak-23 pilot training duties, but the training version of the MiG-15 was preferred due to its better characteristics. In 1957 the Institute of Aviation obtained two aircraft. One was scrapped after damage and the other one was registered SP-GLM and conducted flying tests preceding the first flight of the first Polish-built jet TS-11 *Iskra*. After that, in 1964 it was donated to the Museum, where it was repainted in a fictional military paint scheme.

44 | POLISH AVIATION MUSEUM CRACOW

Yakovlev Yak-23

In March 1947 the Soviet government issued requirements for a new frontline fighter aircraft. The most successful design following those requirements was the MiG-15 swept-wing aircraft by Mikoyan and Gurievich. The Yakovlev bureau designed the straight wing Yak-23 aircraft, based on the previous Yakovlev jets. The new aircraft had a metal monocoque fuselage with stressed skin, which was a great technological advance compared to previous Yakovlev designs, and was powered by the RD-500 engine - a Soviet licence-built Rolls-Royce Derwent V. The Yak-23 made its first flight in June 1947. Despite several shortcomings of the aircraft, production began in 1948. The Yak-23 was expected to perform fighter tasks below 33,000 ft (above was the operational level of the MiG-15). The aircraft was agile, easy to fly and maintain, had a high rate of climb and was able to operate from unpaved airstrips. In early 1950s deliveries to Poland, Romania, Czechoslovakia and Bulgaria began.

Poland was the major foreign Yak-23 operator, using 90 aircraft until the mid 1950s. It was the first jet fighter in Polish Air Force. On November 21st, 1957 Polish test pilot Andrzej Abłamowicz of the Institute of Aviation, flying a civil registered Yak-23, set two class records by climbing 3,000 m in 119 seconds and 6,000 m in 197 seconds.

The displayed aircraft was donated to the Museum in 1964.

POLISH AVIATION MUSEUM CRACOW | 45

Avia B-33

The Ilyushin Il-2 *Shturmovik*, called the "Black Death" by German tank crews, is one of the Second World War's legendary warplanes, which enabled the defeat of the Third Reich. In 1944 its successor the Il-10 appeared, featuring all-metal construction, more effective armament and armour and a more powerful engine. The Il-10 entered service at the end of the war and was widely used against Japanese forces. A couple of years later the Il-10 also saw combat during the Korean war.

In 1951 the Avia – Letnany plant in Czechoslovakia undertook licence production of the Il-10 under the designation Avia B-33. First aircraft entered service the next year. 1,200 aircraft were built, of which almost half were sold to Poland, Hungary, Bulgaria and Romania.

Poland purchased combat B-33 and trainer CB-33 versions. They remained in service until the late 1950s and subsequently most of them were written off and scrapped.

The displayed aircraft, built in 1952, sported numbers 29 and 4 in combat units. After the Aviation Exhibition on the 20th anniversary of the People's Republic of Poland it was donated to the Polish Aviation Museum.

POLISH AVIATION MUSEUM CRACOW

Zlin Z-26 *Trener*

The Zlin Z-26 is a two-seat low wing trainer aircraft of mixed construction, designed in 1947 in Czechoslovakia by Karel Thomas. It is the first of the long line of Zlin trainer and aerobatic aircraft, ending with the Zlin-726 model.

Between 1949 and 1951 113 Zlin Z-26s with wooden wings were built. In 1952 Poland purchased 38 aircraft, which were used for pilot training and aerobatics until 1974. During the 1970s they were replaced by the Zlin-526F aircraft with more powerful engines and retractable landing gear.

The displayed aircraft, serial number 640, SP-ARM, is the only Zlin Z-26 surviving in Poland. Until 1974 it was used by Cracow Aero Club, from where it was retired to the Museum.

POLISH AVIATION MUSEUM CRACOW | 47

Aero-145

The Aero-145 is a twin engine executive and medical transport aircraft, developed in 1959 in Czechoslovakia at the SPP Kunovice company as the successor to the earlier model Aero Ae-45, with more powerful M-332 engines. 150 aircraft were built, mainly for export to the USSR. Production ceased after the introduction of the L-200 Morava. They were operated mainly by medical transport units until the late 1970s.

The displayed aircraft, serial number 172011, registered SP-LXH, was built in 1959. It flew with the Medical Air Transport Unit in Zielona Góra. In 1980 it was retired to the Museum.

48 | POLISH AVIATION MUSEUM CRACOW

Aero L-60E *Brigadyr*

Aero L-60 *Brigadyr* is a multi-role aircraft designed in 1950s in Czechoslovakia for the Ministry of Defense. It was a successor to the Fi-156 *Storch* and its design is based on the German aircraft – a metal four seat aircraft in high-wing configuration with braced wings. The design studies were conducted at the Aero plant in Prague under the supervision of Ondrei Nemec. Three prototypes were built. The first one, designated XL-60, first flew in 1953. The third prototype, designed by Zdenek Rublic, which was the pattern for series production first flew in 1955. Production began at the Orličan plant in Choclnia and totalled 250 aircraft built between 1956 and 1960. *Brigadyrs* were exported to many countries, including East Germany, USSR, New Zealand, Argentina and Egypt. Several versions - executive, medical and agricultural - were developed. Trials with a military version, designated L-160, were also conducted, but were later abandoned. *Brigadyr*'s main deficiency was the unreliable Praga Doris six cylinder engine.

In 1957 the Polish Ministry of Health purchased three L-60F aircraft for medical air transport. The displayed aircraft, serial number 150723, SP-FXA, was donated by the Medical Air Transport Unit in Cracow on January 6th, 1974. *Brigadyrs* are still used by aero clubs in the Czech Republic and Slovakia for towing gliders and dropping parachutists. Most of them were retrofitted with more reliable and powerful AI-14 radial engines.

Aero L-200A *Morava*

The Aero L-200 *Morava* is a five seat twin-engine all-metal low wing aircraft, used as executive and flying ambulance, designed in 1957 at the LET company at Kunovice, Czechoslovakia as the successor of the Aero-145. Series production commenced in 1960 and until 1964 367 aircraft were built, the L-200A (with two blade propellers) and L-200D (with three blade propellers) versions. They were exported in large numbers to the USSR, Yugoslavia and Poland. In Poland they were operated by medical transport units and large state enterprises as executive aircraft.

The displayed aircraft, serial number 170409, SP-NXA, was donated to the Museum in 1984 by the Central Medical Air Transport Unit in Warsaw.

50 | POLISH AVIATION MUSEUM CRACOW

Bücker Bü-131 Jungmann

Bücker Bü-131 *Jungmann* is a two seat biplane trainer, designed in 1933 in Germany by Swedish engineer Anders Andersson. Although the *Jungmann* was designed over 70 years ago, it still has devoted fans throughout the world. Production commenced in 1935. In 1936 the *Jungmann* entered service as a basic trainer in the NSFK (*Nationalsozialistischer Fliegerkorps*) and *Luftwaffe*. It was especially suitable for fighter pilot training. Many German fighter aces, for example Erich Hartmann, made their debut in the air in a *Jungmann*. The *Jungmann* was also licence-built in large numbers in Switzerland as the Do/Bü-131, in Spain as the CASA1.131 and Japan, where they served for Army pilot training as the Ki-86 and the Navy as the K9W1 *Momiji*. Before the war in Czechoslovakia the Tatra company licence-built 10 aircraft, designated T-131. During the war the Germans produced *Jungmanns* at the Aero factory at Prague. The Czechs continued production after the war – 200 aircraft were built between 1946 and 1949 under the designation Aero C-104, with the Walter Minor 4-III engine. Nowadays the *Jungmann* is one the most popular vintage aircraft, many of these machines flying throughout the world. There are many people willing to possess one, so the aircraft is still in production. Between 1989 and 1995 a group of aviation specialists led by Janusz Karasiewicz built four replicas. The first one first flew in 1994. These aircraft had no baggage compartment and were powered by Walter Minor carburettor engines. In 1995 the Historic Aircraft Service company was established and undertook production from Bücker licence under the designation Bücker T-131PA *Jungmann*, based on the original German documentation and type certificate from 1937.

The displayed aircraft remained in Poland after the war. It underwent overhaul at the District Aviation Works, registered SP-AFO, and was operated by the Poznań Aero Club from 1946 to 1955.

Messerschmitt Bf 109G

The Messerschmitt Bf 109 is one of the most important aircraft of the Second World War. Throughout the war it was the main type of *Luftwaffe* fighter. It was designed by Willy Messerschmitt at the Bayerische Flugzeugwerke (BFW) at Augsburg for the contest for a new fighter aircraft announced by the RLM in 1934. The design was based on an earlier Messerschmitt, the Bf 108 *Taifun* tourer, an all-metal low wing monoplane with retractable landing gear, developed for the Challenge competition in 1934. The prototype of the Bf 109, powered by a British Rolls-Royce Kestrel engine (Daimler and Junkers engines destined for the new fighter were not available at that time) first flew in 1935. In 1937 production of the Bf 109B version began. As early as the beginning of 1937 pre-production aircraft were sent to Spain to be tested in combat by the Condor Legion during the Spanish Civil War. They were soon joined by production aircraft. Subsequent Jumo 210-powered versions were the Bf 109C and Bf 109D. In late 1938 the Bf 109E version, powered by the DB-601 engine and armed with two 7.92 mm MG-17 machine guns in the fuselage and two in the wings (in later sub-variants replaced by 20 mm MG FF cannons) entered production. The E version became the main type of *Luftwaffe* fighter from 1939 to early 1941. In October 1940 the first aircraft of the Bf 109F version, from which the second generation of the Bf 109 begins, entered service. The new fighter featured redesigned wings with rounded tips and no armament and redesigned nose with enlarged spinner. The armament comprised two 7.92 mm MG-17 machine guns in the nose and a 20 mm MG 151 cannon between the cylinder blocks, firing through the propeller hub. Subsequent development versions were the Bf 109G and Bf 109K, powered by DB-605 engines. In total, 33,984 aircraft of all versions were built. Based on the Bf 109 design, the Avia S.99 and S.199 in Czechoslovakia and Hispano HA 1109 and HA.1112 *Buchon* fighters in Spain were developed.

The displayed aircraft, serial number 163306, red 3 is a G-6, the Bf 109 variant built in largest numbers – ca 12,000 aircraft were built. Its service life was very short. It was rolled out of the factory on 11th May 1944 and was assigned to *Jagdgruppe* West, a fighter training unit based at Jaworze (Gabbert) in northern Poland. On the morning of 28th May 1944 *Fw.* Ernst Pleiners took off on a training flight. Just after take-off the engine cut off and the aircraft ditched in nearby Lake Trzebuń. In 2000 the wreckage was recovered and restored by the employees of the Polish Eagles Foundation. The aircraft is the property of the Foundation and is on temporary lease to the Museum in exchange for an airworthy Yak-18.

SP-GIL

In 1947 at the Technical Institute of Aviation (in 1948 renamed Central Institute of Aviation) engineers Zbigniew Brzoska, Bronisław Żurakowski and Tadeusz Chyliński began studies on a new type of aircraft - a helicopter. In 1949 the design was ready and the prototype was built. The fuselage was a welded steel tube structure covered with fabric and aluminum panels. The tail boom was made of wood. The main rotor was of the Hiller type, with stabilizer blades. The powerplant was a 100 hp German Hirth HM 504 engine and some elements of a German Zundapp motorbike were used in the tail rotor gear. The helicopter did not receive an official name, only the registration SP-GIL. Flight tests began in 1950, and were conducted by Bronisław Żurakowski, who had never piloted a helicopter before. The tests lasted until 1956. Several failures and accidents occurred, after which the helicopter was modified and continued tests.

SP-GIL was a pioneer construction (in those days virtually nobody in Poland had any idea about helicopters), built in a war-ruined country in extremely difficult conditions, yet it performed well. Unfortunately, studies on helicopters in Poland were cancelled. The real beginning of the rotorcraft era in Polish aviation was the beginning of licence production of the Mi-1 in 1956.

JK-1 *Trzmiel*

In 1955 the Institute of Aviation began studies on an experimental jet-propelled observation helicopter for the army. The helicopter, which was given the name *Trzmiel* (bumblebee) was powered by two ramjet engines mounted on the rotor blade tips. The fuselage was a welded steel tube structure with skid undercarriage. Ground tests commenced in 1957 and problems with rotor blade flutter occurred. During one of the tests, one of the engines broke apart and killed the pilot. The tests were continued with the second prototype, but were cancelled after another accident. The analysis of the accidents and research on similar constructions conducted in other countries proved that the design was not practical. The Bumblebee had never flown, remaining only a technical experiment.

SM-1

Helicopters were operationally used for the first time by the Germans and Americans during the Second World War. After the war in the USSR Mikhail Mil began studies on helicopters. In 1948 the prototype of the Mi-1, powered by a specially designed AI-26W engine, made its first flight. In 1952 the helicopter entered production. 1,013 machines were built. In 1957 the improved versions Mi-1A and Mi-1M were developed.

In 1956 the Polish factory WSK Świdnik undertook licence production of the Mi-1 under the designation SM-1 and the WSK Rzeszów started production of the AI-26 engine under the designation Trion Lit-3. In 1959 an improved version SM-1/600, based on the Mi-1A, entered production. Several utility variants were developed - dual control trainer, ambulance, flying crane, and agricultural. In 1960 a multipurpose version, the SM-1W equivalent to Mi-1M, entered production. The last production version was the SM-1Wb, fitted with hydraulic control servo and rotor blades with 800 hour total service time. The SM-1 remained in production until 1965. 1,597 machines were built, most of them exported to the USSR.

The Mi-1 was the first Soviet helicopter produced in large numbers. In Poland the SM-1 started the era of production and use of helicopters. They remained in service until 1983. Thanks to the production of the SM-1, PZL Świdnik became one of the world's largest helicopter manufacturers.

The displayed helicopter, serial number S10-1003, SP-SAD, is the third SM-1 built. From 1957 till 1973 it was used by the Institute of Aviation for testing various devices, including a small wing. It was retired to the Museum in 1973. The helicopter was delivered by test pilot Ryszard Witkowski, who performed the majority of the tests in SP-SAD.

54 | POLISH AVIATION MUSEUM CRACOW

SM-2

The Mi-1 had a powerful engine, which enabled carriage of more payload or passengers. Basing on its propulsion system, between 1957 and 59 at WSK Świdnik a new fuselage with larger, glazed cockpit with 5 seats and opening front section, was designed. Large sliding door on both sides of fuselage enabled rescue operations with the use of a hoist. The new helicopter was designated SM-2. 85 machines were built. They were operated by military and later medical aviation until 1979. A few SM-2s were exported to Czechoslovakia.

The displayed helicopter, registered SP-SAP, is a prototype used as a factory helicopter until 1975.

Mil Mi-2URP

In the late 1950s in the USSR studies on a successor to the Mi-1 began. The new helicopter had to be turbine powered and capable of carrying 8 people. The Klimov design bureau began studies on a GTD-350 turboshaft engine, based on the American Allison 250. The prototype of the W-2 helicopter first flew in 1961. Series production, under the designation Mi-2, began in 1963. In 1964 Poland was granted the licence and in 1965 production at the WSK Świdnik factory began. WSK Rzeszów undertook production of the GTD-350 engines. The Mi-2 is a very versatile machine. In civil aviation they are used for medical rescue, transport, pilot training, patrolling and agriculture. Mi-2s are also operated by the police and border guards. Several military versions were designed: transport/medevac, passenger, dual control trainer, chemical reconnaissance/smokescreen.

At the end of the 1960s analysis of successful combat use of helicopters by the Americans in Vietnam started studies on armed strike versions. Three versions were designed: Mi-2US, armed with machine guns, Mi-2URN armed with rocket launchers and Mi-2URP armed with a cannon and *Malutka* guided anti-tank missiles. The Museum possesses the Mi-2 helicopters of the armed URP version, Mi-2Ch chemical reconnaissance/smokescreen, transport/passenger version, civil agricultural version, and a prototype of the troop carrier Mi-2M2

56 | POLISH AVIATION MUSEUM CRACOW

WWS *Wrona bis*

The *Wrona* (Crow) is a wooden single seat elementary training glider, designed in 1932 by Antoni Kocjan. It was a very successful design, which quickly entered service in all gliding schools in Poland. It was built by the Glider Workshop of Antoni Kocjan in Warsaw and under licence by different small workshops at gliding clubs in various towns. In 1934 a modified *Wrona bis* version, with the wingspan enlarged by 0.5 m, was developed. Apart from the Kocjan Workshop, these gliders were licence-built by the Scout Glider Workshops in Warsaw, Silesian Glider Workshop in Bielsko-Biała and the Military Glider Workshops in Cracow. In total, 450 were built. They were also licence built in Estonia, Finland, Palestine and Yugoslavia.

The displayed glider was built by the Military Glider Workshops in Cracow. It is the only surviving one, stored in secrecy during the Second World War. After the war it was overhauled at the Institute of Soaring in Bielsko-Biała and used for test flights until 1950, registered SP-127. In 1963 it was retired to the Museum.

WWS-2 ŻABA

The *Żaba* (Frog) is a is a wooden single-seat elementary training glider, designed in 1937 by Wacław Czerwiński at the Military Glider Workshops in Cracow. It proved to be a successful and safe design. An oleo strut between the fuselage and skid was applied and the seat is especially formed to protect the pilot's spine in case of a crash landing. The *Żabas* were used by gliding schools throughout Poland. 140 were built in Cracow and Lvov until the outbreak of the Second World War.

The displayed glider was built by the Military Glider Workshops in Cracow. It is the only surviving one, stored in secrecy during the Second World War in Krosno. After the war it was overhauled at the Institute of Soaring in Bielsko-Biała and used for test flights until 1950. In 1964 it was retired to the Museum.

IS-A SALAMANDRA

The WWS-1 *Salamandra* (Salamander) glider was designed in 1936 by Wacław Czerwiński at the Military Glider Workshops in Cracow. It was an intermediate (between the elementary and more advanced training) glider of wooden construction. *Salamandras* were built in large numbers for Polish gliding schools before the Second World War, they were also exported to France, Estonia, Finland, Hungary, Romania and Yugoslavia. One glider survived the war in Goleszów and on its basis Marian Gracz and Rudolf Matz reconstructed the technical documentation at the Institute of Soaring in Bielsko-Biała, modifying the design and production technology. In 1946 series production began. The first batch of five gliders was built in Bielsko-Biała. Subsequent batches of improved versions, designated *Salamandra* 48, 49, 53 and the export version 53A for China were built in Jeżów Sudecki. Production totalled 264 gliders. The *Salamandras* were used for training from 1947 until 1961.

The displayed glider, serial number 003, SP-322, was built in 1946 in Bielsko-Biała as the third of the first production batch. It was used until 1955 and then retired to the Museum of Technology in Warsaw, from where it was handed over to the Polish Aviation Museum in 1963.

CHAPTER 2: 1930S TO THE PRESENT

IS-1 *Sęp bis*

The IS-1 *Sęp* (Vulture) *bis* is the first high performance glider designed in Poland after the Second World War. It is of all-wooden construction. The prototype first flew in June 1947. A batch of five gliders was built, used by the top Polish glider pilots for competition and performance flying. In 1952 Ryszard Bittner made a 499 km long flight in a *Sęp*.

The displayed glider, serial number 011, SP-552, was used from 1948 to 1962. In this aircraft Irena Kempówna set a national speed record of 36.8 km/h over a 100 km course to a declared goal and an international speed record of 50 km/h over a triangular course of 100 km. In 1964 the glider was retired to the Museum by the SZD works.

SZD-18 *Czajka*

The SZD-18 *Czajka* (lapwing) is a single-seat training glider of wooden construction, designed by Tadeusz Grudzieński. The design, number X-11, won the competition for a new training glider announced in 1955. Technical documentation was done by a team supervised by Władysław Okarmus at SZD Bielsko in 1956. The prototype, registered SP-1640, made its first flight on 30th November 1956 with Adam Zientek at the controls. It was the best single seat training glider designed in Poland, but the change of the pilot training system from single to dual control, implemented at that time, meant that its development ended at the prototype stage. The only *Czajka* flew with the Warsaw Aero Club, from which it was retired to the Museum in 1966.

POLISH AVIATION MUSEUM CRACOW | 59

IS-B *Komar* 49

The wooden training glider *Komar* (Mosquito) was designed and built by Antoni Kocjan in 1933. In 1937 an improved *Komar-bis* version, with increased wing stiffness, was developed. It was an outstanding glider. On 13–14th May 1937, Wanda Modlibowska set a world record of unpowered flight duration of 24 hours and 14 minutes. Until the outbreak of the Second World War 67 gliders were built. They were also licence-built in Bulgaria, Estonia, Finland, France, Yugoslavia, Palestine and Romania.

In 1947 at the Gliding Institute in Bielsko-Biała Marian Wasilewski adapted the design to post-war requirements, based on plans given by Kocjan's widow. The first post-war *Komar* flew on 16th January 1948. During 1948 five gliders, designated *Komar* 48, were built. An improved version designated *Komar* 49 was subsequently developed and 18 were built. They had very good characteristics and remained in use until 1965. In a *Komar* 48 Stanisław Wielgus established an unpowered flight duration record of 35 hours and 14 minutes on 19-20th October 1949.

The displayed glider, with registration SP-985, was built in 1950 in Jeżów Sudecki and was operated by Szczecin Aero Club and Mountain Gliding School on the Żar mountain.

IS-4 *Jastrząb*

The IS-4 *Jastrząb* (Hawk) is a wooden aerobatic glider, designed at the Institute of Soaring in Bielsko-Biała in 1949. It is distinguished by an exceptionally rugged construction and thus very high maximum speed, exceeding 450 km/h in a dive. During 1952-1953 35 were built in Bielsko-Biała and Krosno. Thanks to the solid construction they remained in service until the late 1960s.

The displayed glider, serial number 017, SP-1391, was operated by the Krosno Aero Club from 1953 till 1964, from where it was retired to the aircraft exhibition on the 20th anniversary of the People's Republic of Poland and then to the Museum.

SZD-6X Nietoperz

SZD-6X *Nietoperz* (Bat) is an experimental glider of tailless layout, built as a single unit. It was used for operational evaluation of this type of construction and studies on the drag directional control system without a vertical tailplane, with split outer ailerons serving as a rudder. The glider was developed by engineers Władysław Nowakowski and Justyn Sandauer at the Gliding Institute in Bielsko-Biała, renamed in 1950 the Gliding Experimental Works. The *Nietoperz* first flew on 12th January 1951 with Adam Zientek at the controls. The tow plane was a PWS-26, piloted by Tadeusz Góra, the first Polish holder of the Lilienthal Medal. Flying tests lasted until 1959 and then the *Nietoperz* was donated to Technical Museum in Warsaw. It was extremely difficult to fly and required exceptional safety measures during the test flights. A directional control system similar to the one tested on the *Nietoperz* is presently used in the B-2 Spirit American stealth bomber.

SZD-9bis Bocian 1A

The SZD-9 *Bocian* (Stork) 1A was designed at the SZD in Bielsko-Biała in 1952 as two-seat high performance glider. It was then one of the world's most modern gliders. The improved version SZD-9*bis Bocian* 1A entered production at the 2nd Air Sports Production Facility in Jeżów Sudecki in 1953. Subsequent development variants were designated *Bocian* 1B, 1C and 1D. 29 world records were set in *Bocian* gliders, including climb to 11,680 m, out-and-return distance 544 km, and speed 108 km/h over a triangular course of 100 km. In the second half of 1960 the *Bocians* were no longer suitable for performance flying and the *Bocian* 1E version for basic training was developed. Production lasted until 1976. 645 were built, of which many were sold to 27 countries. *Bocians* have remained in use in Polish aero clubs until the present.

The displayed glider, serial number P-231, SP-1358, was operated by the Cracow Aero Club from 1953 to 1974.

IS-C ŻURAW

The *Żuraw* (Crane) is a two-seat training glider, based on the design of the German DFS *Kranich* II glider, developed by Hans Jacobs in the late 1930s. It was the glider built in the largest numbers in Germany before the Second World War. After the war at the Institute of Soaring in Bielsko-Biała the technical documentation was recreated on the basis of surviving gliders. The prototype of the Polish version first flew on April 22nd, 1952. Series production was undertaken by the 4th Air Sports Production Facility in Gdansk. 51 gliders were built between 1952 and 1953. They were used until the mid 1960s.

The displayed glider, serial number 009, SP-1213, was used from 1962 to 1964 by the Gliwice Aero Club.

SZD-10BIS CZAPLA

The SZD-10*bis Czapla* (Heron) is a two-seat wooden training glider, developed during 1952-1953 at the SZD in Bielsko-Biała after the decision to switch to a dual control training scheme. The prototype first flew in 1953 and after numerous modifications the SZD-10*bis* version entered production in 1955. They were built by the 5th Air Sports Production Facility in Krosno and Military Repair Works in Łódź. They were the main type of basic training glider in Polish aero clubs. They remained in use until the early 1980s. They were exported to Finland and Turkey.

The displayed glider, serial number 124, SP-1477, was operated by the Cracow Aero Club from 1956 till 1972.

SZD-8bis Jaskółka

The SZD-8*bis Jaskółka* (Swallow) is a wooden high performance glider, developed at the SZD in Bielsko-Biała in 1951. The prototype first flew on 21st September 1951. The SZD-8*bis* version entered production in 1953. Based on the experience gained during the operation of that version, subsequent variants were developed – *bis* E, *bis* Z with water ballast, export *bis* O, *ter* Z with metal airbrakes, and simplified *ter* ZO without water ballast tanks. In 1954 a successful experimental version SZD-14X, featuring a V-tail, was developed.

The Swallow was an exceptionally successful design, 17 world records were set on this type. During the 1950s it was the most popular type of high performance glider in Poland. 135 gliders in all versions were built, many of which were sold abroad.

The displayed glider, serial number 114, SP-1335, was operated by the Cracow Aero Club from 1954 to 1969 and then donated to the Museum.

SZD –17X Jaskółka L

The SZD –17X *Jaskółka* L is a development version of the *Jaskółka* glider, based on the SZD-14X version, but actually a totally new design. It is a high performance glider designed for strong thermals conditions, featuring a laminar flow airfoil, water ballast and V-tail, designed especially for the 1956 World Gliding Championships. The prototype first flew on 9th March 1956. Four gliders were built, although they did not take part in the championships for fear of losing in case of weak thermals during the competition. They were used in Poland for competition and performance flying.

The displayed glider, serial number 174, SP-1506, was used between 1956 and 1977. On 9th May 1956 Tadeusz Góra set a speed record in a course to a declared goal.

SZD-12 *Mucha* 100

The SZD-12 *Mucha* (Fly) 100 is a wooden training and high performance glider, designed in 1952-1953 as the successor to one of the most popular Polish post-war gliders, the IS-2 *Mucha*. The *Mucha* 100 entered production in the 5th Air Sports Production Facility in Krosno, subsequent batches were also built in Gdańsk and Wrocław. In 1958 an upgraded *Mucha* 100A version entered production. It was a successful glider liked by its pilots. Production totalled 350, of which 70 were sold to Switzerland, Italy, East Germany, China, USSR. China undertook licence production.

The displayed glider, serial number 95, SP-1463, was operated by the Cracow Aero Club from 1955 to 1978 and was retired to the Museum.

SZD-22C *Mucha* Standard

The SZD-22C *Mucha* Standard is another extensive modification of the *Mucha* glider. The prototype first flew on February 10th, 1958. In the same year Adam Witek took first place in the World Gliding Championships in Leszno in the prototype SP-1749. The *Mucha* Standard is distinguished by superb flying characteristics. 286 were built in the A, B and C variants. During the 1960s and 1970s it was the main type of training and high performance glider in Polish aero clubs. Many still fly. More than 90 were sold to Austria, Australia, Belgium, France, Finland, Germany, Sweden, Mexico, USA, Switzerland and other countries.

SZD-15 *Sroka*

The SZD-15 *Sroka* (Magpie) is a wooden training glider, the successor of the *Komar* glider. The prototype first flew in February 1956, and in 1957 production started in the 5th Air Sports Production Facility in Krosno. 20 were built. These gliders were already obsolete while being designed. They remained in use until the mid 1970s.

The displayed glider, serial number 299, SP-1726, was operated from 1957 to 1975 by the Bielsko-Biała Aero Club and then donated to the Museum.

SZD-21-2B *Kobuz 3*

The design of the *Kobuz* (Hobby) aerobatic glider, initially named Falcon, was developed in the early 1960s to replace the *Jastrząb* (Hawk) glider, designed in 1949. The prototype SZD-21 *Kobuz 1* first flew on 3rd June 1961. It did not have good flight characteristics and was modified to the SZD-21-2 *Kobuz 2* version. The first flight in May 1962 showed no significant improvement. During tests of the subsequent version *Kobuz* 2A test pilot Sławomir Makaruk was killed. Finally the third version, the SZD-21-2B *Kobuz 3* with modified nose and wings, proved to be successful and entered production. 31 gliders were built. Polish pilots have won many international glider aerobatic competitions in *Kobuz 3* gliders, but the end of the glider's career was tragic. During the World Glider Aerobatic Championship in 1989 at Hockenheim, West Germany, a *Kobuz* piloted by Krzysztof Wyskiel lost its wings because moisture had weakened their wooden construction. After the crash the type was retired. Shortly after it was replaced by the Swift glider, designed by Edward Margański.

SZD-25A Lis

The SZD-25 *Lis* (Fox) is a training and high performance glider of mixed construction. The wings from the *Mucha* Standard glider were utilised, with a metal fuselage, covered with fabric in the forward section, based on the SZD-16 *Gil* design. The prototype first flew in 1960. After necessary modifications the SZD-25A version entered production in the 5th Air Sports Production Facility in Krosno. 30 were built, of which 12 were sold abroad.

The displayed glider, serial number 740, SP-2356, was operated by the Piotrków Aero Club from 1962 to 1981 and retired to the Museum.

SZD-19-2A Zefir 2A

The SZD-19-2A *Zefir* (Zephyr) 2A is a wooden high performance open class glider. The *Zefir* 1 prototype of very sophisticated construction was being designed for the 1958 World Gliding Championships in Leszno, but it made the first flight after the competition. Based on the experience gained on it, the *Zefir* 2 of simplified construction was developed. Its prototype first flew in March 1960. In the same year Edward Makula and Jerzy Popiel took second and third places in the World Gliding Championships in Cologne. In 1962 the *Zefir* 2A production version with modified tail made the first flight. In 1963 Edward Makula and Jerzy Popiel took first and second places in the World Gliding Championships in Junin, Argentina in *Zefir* 2As. Edward Makula made then a 717.5 km open distance flight. 20 *Zefir* 2A gliders were built. Some of them were redesignated *Zefir* 2B after modification of the brake chute.

The displayed glider, SP-2371, was donated to the Museum by the Wrocław Aero Club in 1989.

SZD-43 *Orion*

The SZD-43 *Orion* is a high performance glider of mixed construction (wood, metal and fibreglass), developed during 1970 – 1971. Two prototypes were built, in which Jan Wróblewski took first and Franciszek Kępka third places in the World Gliding Championships in Vrsac, Yugoslavia in 1972. The *Orion* did not enter production, because simultaneously the much modern, all fibreglass *Jantar* glider was developed.

Swift S-1

The Swift composite glider was designed by Edward Margański and Jerzy Cisowski as the successor of the *Kobuz* glider, which was retired after the crash in 1989. The displayed glider, with single piece wing, initially designated *Akrobat*, is the first prototype which first flew on 11th January 1990. The first participation of the Swift in the World Championship was a sensation. A Polish-Swiss company, Swift Ltd, undertook series production. 35 gliders were built. Nowadays the Swift and another design of Edward Margański, the MDM Fox, are the world's most popular aerobatic gliders.

POLISH AVIATION MUSEUM CRACOW | 67

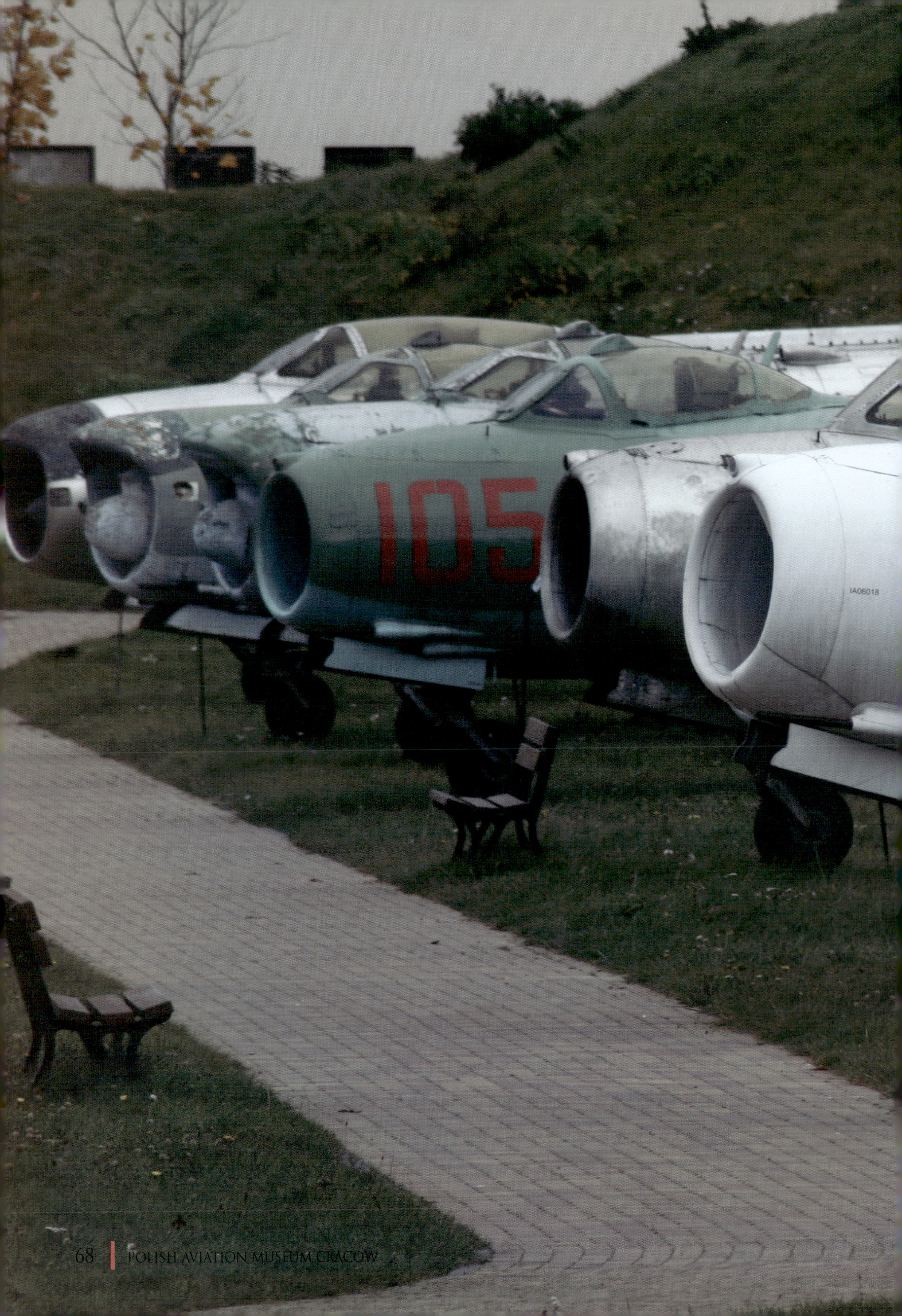
105
IA06018

Chapter 3:
The open air exhibition and MiG Alley

In the open air exhibition the largest aircraft in the Museum's collection, combat jets, passenger and transport airplanes and helicopters are displayed. Among them the executive aircraft of the First Secretaries of the Polish United Labour Party – the Il-14 of Władysław Gomułka and the Yak-40 of Edward Gierek - stand out. The latter was witness to the political changes in Poland, carrying aboard the leaders of communist and then independent Poland. The oldest aircraft, built during the Second World War, is the Lisunov Li-2, Soviet licence-built version of the Douglas DC-3/C-47. Next to it stands one of the most grotesque constructions in the history of aviation, the M-15 *Belfegor* jet agricultural aircraft, a failed Polish-Soviet design from the mid 1970s.

The main part of the open air exhibition, which is the biggest attraction for fans of Cold War era aviation, are the combat jets, grouped primarily on so-called MiG Alley. They are Soviet and Polish aircraft, operated by the Polish Air Force since the early 1950s. Among them are the Lim-1, Lim-2 and Lim-5 (MiG-15s and MiG-17s licence-built in Poland), the Lim-6*bis* Polish attack aircraft, based on the MiG-17 design, MiG-19PM, the first supersonic aircraft in Polish Air Force, and the MiG-21 family – all versions of the aircraft which for almost 40 years was the main type of fighter in Poland. Next to them stand the Su-7 nuclear bombers, which in case of an East-West clash were expected to lead the way for the Warsaw Pact forces in northern Germany. There are also their successors with variable wing geometry, the Su-20 and Su-22.

The newest part of the collection, which has been developed recently, comprises aircraft from the other side of the Iron Curtain. In 2009, on the occasion of the 60th anniversary of NATO and the 10th anniversary of the entry of Poland, an exhibition of aircraft operated by NATO member countries opened. The first exhibits of the collection are the Dassault Mirage V strike aircraft donated by the Belgian Air Force and Lockheed F-104S Starfighter, donated by the Italian Air Force. An exhibit with an exceptional history is the MiG-29UB, retired to the Museum in April 2008. The aircraft was delivered to the air force of the German Democratic Republic in the late 1980s. After Germany had been reunited the MiG-29s were taken over by the *Bundesluftwaffe*, as the first type of Soviet aircraft operated by a NATO member country. The German MiG-29s were operated by JG 73 *Steinhoff* at Laage.

In 2002 the Germans decided to retire the MiG-29s. They were sold to Poland for a token sum of 1 euro. After necessary overhauls they were assigned to the 41st Tactical Air Squadron at Malbork. Aircraft number 4115 was retired in 2007 and donated to the Museum.

Lim-1

The Lim-1 is a licence-built version of the MiG-15 fighter, distinguished by its participation in the Korean War. It was the first jet aircraft to enter series production in Poland.

Studies on the original pattern began two years after the end of the Second World War. The Soviet government issued an order for a new fighter aircraft. As a response, the Mikoyan Design Bureau developed the S-1, S-2 and S-3 experimental aircraft with swept wings, powered by British Rolls-Royce Nene and Nene II engines. The S-3 showed excellent flight characteristics and entered production in 1948 as the MiG-15, powered by the RD-45F engine, which was a clone of the Nene II. 1,344 aircraft were built during 1949 – 1950. Just after the MiG-15 had entered service, it was extensively used in combat during the Korean War. Its main opponent was the F-86 Sabre, to which the MiG-15 was superior in speed, climb and armament.

In 1952 the WSK Mielec plant undertook the licence production under the designation Lim-1 (abbreviation for Licence Fighter 1). 227 were built up to 1954. The RD-45F engine was built at the WSK Rzeszów plant as the Lis-1 (abbreviation for Licence Engine 1). Between 1951 and 1954, 821 aircraft were built in Czechoslovakia. The Polish Air Force operated aircraft of domestic, Czech and Soviet production.

Lim–2

In 1950 in the USSR an upgraded version of the MiG-15, with improved fuselage construction and powered by the uprated VK-1 engine was developed. 7,936 were built in the USSR between 1950 and 1952. In early 1953 the first MiG-15*bis* fighters entered service in the Polish Air Force. 500 were licence-built at the WSK Mielec plant between 1954 and 1956 under the designation Lim-2. The WSK Rzeszów plant undertook the licence production of the VK-1 engine as the Lis-2. The last Lim-2s remained in service until the early 1980s in training units.

MiG-15UTI

Two-seat trainer version of the MiG-15, with reduced armament. Its introduction to service improved and accelerated pilot training. Between 1950 and 1959 3,433 aircraft were built in the USSR. Yuri Gagarin was killed in a crash of a MiG-15 UTI in 1968. During 1954-1961 2,013 aircraft were licence built in Czechoslovakia. The Polish Air Force operated 96 aircraft, purchased from both countries. The main feature distinguishing the MiG-15UTI from Polish two seat conversions was a single 12.7 mm machine gun.

72 | POLISH AVIATION MUSEUM CRACOW

SB Lim-2

After withdrawal from combat units, the Lim-1s were modified to two seat trainers, similar to the MiG-15UTI, armed with one 23 mm cannon. During the overhaul the aircraft were retrofitted with the Lis-2 engine and tail section of the Lim-2. After this modification they received the designation SB Lim-2. Two-seat Lims remained in service until the early 1990s. The displayed aircraft, serial number 1A060018, tail number 018, called "The White Lady" was operated by 1st Reconnaissance Squadron of 7th Attack Regiment of Naval Aviation at Siemirowice on the Baltic coast.

SB Lim-2A

In 1965 some SB Lim-1 and SB Lim-2 were modified to an observation and target artillery spotting version and designated SB Lim-1A and SB Lim-2A. The aft cockpit was adapted for the observer, by removal of flight controls and some equipment. The armament was increased to two 23mm cannon. SB Lim-1 were retired from service in 1975 and SB Lim-2A were re-modified again to a training version and designated SB Lim-2M. The displayed aircraft, serial number 27004, tail number 2004, was operated by 1st Reconnaissance Squadron of 7th Attack Regiment of Naval Aviation at Siemirowice.

74 | POLISH AVIATION MUSEUM CRACOW

Lim-5

Lim-5 is a Polish licence-built version of the MiG-17, the successor to the MiG-15. In 1950 in the USSR studies on increasing the MiG-15's speed without changing the powerplant began. To this end a modified wing with 45 degrees in the inner and 42 degrees sweep in the outer part and a modified tailplane were applied. The fuselage was lengthened by 90 cm and a ventral fin under the tail section added. As soon as some technical problems had been eliminated, the aircraft entered production as the MiG-17. 5,467 aircraft were built. In order to improve manoeuverability, the MiG-17F, powered by a VK-1F engine with afterburner, was developed and entered production in 1952. 1,685 aircraft were built.

MiG-17s took part in several conflicts. The most widespread use occurred during the Vietnam war. Thanks to clever tactics the MiGs managed to destroy many much faster and more modern American aircraft.

Between 1956 and 1960 the WSK Mielec factory in Poland built under licence 477 MiG-17F as the Lim-5. The WSK Rzeszów factory undertook production of VK-1F engines as the Lis-5. There also was a version with photo reconnaissance capability, designated Lim-5R (pictured).

Studies on a fighter interceptor version fitted with radar were also conducted. The MiG-17P version with RP-1 radar was designed. It was the first Soviet-built radar-equipped lightweight interceptor. 225 aircraft were built. In 1954 a MiG-17PF version, powered by the WK-1F engine, entered production. Between 1959 and 1960 129 MiG-17PFs were licence-built in Poland as the Lim-5P.

Lim-6bis

In the late 1950s studies on an attack version of the Lim-5 were conducted. Two versions, Lim-5M and Lim-6, with a significant number of modifications were designed. Both were unsuccessful. Finally, in 1962 the Lim-6*bis* was developed, lacking all previous modifications except a brake chute in an underfin container. Weapons load was carried on two underwing pylons.

Lim-5M and Lim-6 aircraft were modified to Lim-6bis standard and entered service in 1963. During 1964 70 brand new aircraft were built, some of them in a reconnaissance version, the Lim-6bisR.

The Lim-5s and Lim-6s remained in service until the early 1990s.

76 | POLISH AVIATION MUSEUM CRACOW

Lim-6MR

In the late 1960s the Lim-5Ps were no longer combat capable as fighter interceptors. In 1971 some were modified to attack aircraft. Additional weapons pylons were installed and the radar was replaced by a battery. The aircraft was designated Lim-6M, and its reconnaissance version Lim-6MR.

CHAPTER 3: THE OPEN AIR EXHIBITION AND MIG ALLEY

POLISH AVIATION MUSEUM CRACOW | 77

Mikoyan MiG-19PM

MiG-19 is a twin engine supersonic jet fighter designed in the USSR during the early 1950s. In 1954 an interceptor version, with radar linked to the gunsight and an IFF interrogator was designed. In 1956 a subsequent version, the MiG-19PM capable of carrying RS-2US air-to-air guided missiles, was developed. The MiG-19 had a rather bad reputation. New technologies applied on this aircraft caused several problems, never completely eliminated despite several modifications.

The Polish Air Force purchased 33 MiG-19s – 19 P and 14 PM versions - delivered in 1958-59, which remained in service until 1974. The MiG-19 was the first supersonic aircraft in Polish aviation.

The MiG-19 was licence-built in Czechoslovakia as the S-105 and in China as the Shenyang F-6. The Q-5 strike aircraft was based on the F-6 design. About 40 F-6s took part in the Vietnam War. One of the top USAF fighter aces, Maj. Robert Lodge, was downed by an F-6 in 1972.

Mikoyan MiG-21

The MiG-21 is the fighter aircraft built in the greatest number after the Second World War, a veteran of various conflicts, of which the Vietnam War is the best known. Despite being obsolete it remains in service in some countries today.

In 1950s in the USSR studies on a supersonic frontline fighter began. The Mikoyan bureau designed the Ye-2 and Ye-2A experimental aircraft with swept wings and the Ye-4 and Ye-5 with delta wing. The Ye-5 was produced in a short series as the MiG-21. Flight tests proved better characteristics of the delta wing, and studies on the Ye-2, Ye-2A, Ye-4 and Ye-5 ceased to focus on the Ye-6, which was a further development of the Ye-5. The Ye-6 with a new R-11F-300 engine first flew in 1958. It entered production in 1959 as the MiG-21F, armed with two 30 mm cannon, bombs and rocket launchers. In 1960 a new version, the MiG-21F-13 (pictured), armed with one cannon and capable of carrying K-13 infrared guided air-to-air missiles (a copy of the American AIM-9 Sidewinder) was developed.

The MiG-21F-13 was licence-built in China, as the Shenyang J-7, and Czechoslovakia. Poland was refused a licence. The Polish Air Force purchased 25 aircraft, delivered 1961-1963, which remained in service until 1973.

A subsequent version was the MiG-21PF, equipped with radar, armed with two radar-homing RS-2US and IR-homing K-13 missiles, with no fixed cannon armament, and with an additional dorsal fuel tank, produced from 1962-1966. The Polish Air Force purchased 84 aircraft, delivered 1964-65, which remained in service until 1989.

The successor to the PF was the MiG-21PFM, produced 1964-1968. Modifications included a new KM-1 ejection seat which led to replacement of the single piece canopy hinged to the front with a windscreen and canopy hinged to the right, enlarged fin and redesigned wings with blown flaps to improve take-off characteristics. A new fire control system was installed, which enabled the aircraft to attack ground targets with bombs and missiles. A ventral provision for a GM-9 gun pod with twin barrel GSh-23 cannon was added. MiGs-21 of the F-13, PF and PFM versions took part in the Vietnam and Israeli/Arab wars.

The Polish Air Force purchased 132 MiG-21PFMs, delivered 1966-1968. It was the version of the MiG-21 operated in the greatest number in Poland.

Mikoyan MiG-21F13

Mikoyan MiG-21PF

Mikoyan MiG-21PFM

The third generation of the MiG-21 was developed based on Vietnam and Israeli/Arab combat experience, which proved the need to increase range and weapons load. The first was the MiG-21R reconnaissance fighter, with enlarged spine housing an additional 340 l tank, and a second pair of underwing pylons plumbed to accept drop tanks. The MiG-21R was fitted with various types of ventral camera pods, underwing ECM pods and upgraded avionics suite. With the pod removed, the aircraft could also serve as missile-only interceptor. Production lasted from 1965 to 1971.

The Polish Air Force purchased 36 aircraft, delivered 1968-1972. They were operated by the 32nd Tactical Reconnaissance Regiment at Sochaczew.

In 1965 a fighter version, the MiG-21S, with dorsal tank housed in an enlarged spine and four underwing weapon/fuel pylons inherited from the R version was developed. The aircraft was fitted with a new RP-22 radar and ASP-PFD gunsight. A subsequent version was the MiG-21SM, powered by the new R-13-300 engine and with a built-in GSh-23 ventral cannon. An export version, the MiG-21M, with the powerplant, radar and rocket missiles of the PFM was developed and produced from 1968-1971. Poland purchased 36 aircraft. The export MiG-21MF (pictured), with the engine and radar of the SM, was subsequently developed and produced 1970-1975. Poland purchased 120 MiG-21MF aircraft, delivered between 1972 and 1975, operated until 2002.

Mikoyan MiG-21MF

POLISH AVIATION MUSEUM CRACOW

CHAPTER 3: THE OPEN AIR EXHIBITION AND MIG ALLEY

Mikoyan MiG-21M

Mikoyan MiG-21R

POLISH AVIATION MUSEUM CRACOW | 81

MiG-21 - the Fourth Generation

The experience gained during the Middle East and Vietnam conflicts proved the need to improve the combat characteristics of the MiG-21 at low and medium altitudes and increase the range while carrying the same load of ordnance. The fourth generation was developed, the MiG-21*bis*, produced 1972-1982. 2,030 aircraft were built.

Externally the aircraft resembled the MiG-21MF airframe. Major changes involved redesigned internal fuselage structure of reduced weight and increased durability, internal fuel tanks of increased capacity, new R-25-300 engine with a special mode, called the "second afterburner", improving performance at low altitudes, and RSBN instrumental navigation and landing system. Armament was supplemented with highly maneuverable R-60 infra-red homing missile.

The MiG-21*bis* was used in combat in Afghanistan, and by the Iraqi Air Force during the Iraq-Iran war from 1980 to 1988, and the Gulf War in 1991. During the Iraq–Iran war a number of MiG-21s were modified to accept the French Matra Magic missile.

Despite modifications, the main deficiencies of the MiG-21 like short range, insufficient ordnance load and poor radar characteristics could not be eliminated.

Poland purchased 72 aircraft, delivered 1980–1981. They were retired from service in 2003.

Mikoyan MiG-21bis

Mikoyan MiG-21bis

82 | POLISH AVIATION MUSEUM CRACOW

CHAPTER 3: THE OPEN AIR EXHIBITION AND MIG ALLEY

MIKOYAN MIG-21BIS

MiG-21U

Mig-21U was the trainer version of first generation MiG-21 (F and F-13 versions), produced 1962-1968. The Polish Air Force operated 11 aircraft, delivered 1965-66, withdrawn from service in 1990.

POLISH AVIATION MUSEUM CRACOW | 83

MiG-21US

Trainer version of second generation MiG-21 (PF and PFM), with cockpit instrumentation similar to the PF/PFM, KM-1 ejection seats and blown flaps. Produced 1966-1970.

The Polish Air Force operated 12 aircraft, delivered 1969 – 1970.

MiG-21UM

Two-seat training version of the third generation MiG-21 (SM, M, MF, R). Production lasted from 1971 till 1985 and totalled more than 1,000 aircraft. The UM version differed from its predecessor, the MiG-21US, by its upgraded equipment. Poland purchased 54 aircraft, delivered 1971–1981, operated until 2003.

84 | POLISH AVIATION MUSEUM CRACOW

CHAPTER 3: THE OPEN AIR EXHIBITION AND MIG ALLEY

Mikoyan MiG-23MF

The MiG-23 was designed as a successor to the MiG-21. Variable geometry wings, then recognized as optimal, were used. The prototype first flew in 1967. The first series production version, the MiG-23S, did not satisfy its users. In 1972 an improved version, the MiG-23M, with all the faults of the MiG-23S removed, made its first flight. Two export versions were developed: the MiG-23MF for Warsaw Pact countries and the MiG-23MS, with reduced equipment, for Third World countries. A two-seat trainer version, the MiG-23UB for type conversion, was also built. In 1971 an attack version entered production, the MiG-23B, which was a base for development of a new aircraft, the MiG-27. In 1976 a modernized version, the MiG-23ML, with a new type of engine and upgraded avionics was developed. It remained in production until 1985. NATO codename for the MiG-23 was "Flogger".

The Polish Air Force purchased 36 MiG-23MF and 6 MiG-23UB aircraft, delivered 1978-1982. They were operated by the 28th Fighter Regiment in Słupsk. Their main tasks were patrol missions over the Baltic Sea. After the disbandment of the unit in 1999 the MiG-23s were retired from service.

POLISH AVIATION MUSEUM CRACOW | 85

Mikoyan MiG-29UB

The MiG-29 is currently the main fighter type in the Polish Air Force. The first aircraft were delivered to Poland in 1989. The displayed aircraft is a MiG-29UB two–seat combat trainer, without radar and with reduced combat capabilities. It was formerly operated by the *Lufstreitkräfte der NVA* (air force of the German Democratic Republic) and then the *Bundesluftwaffe*. In 2003 German MiG-29s were sold to Poland for 1 euro. They entered service with the 41th Tactical Air Squadron at Malbork. Some highest–time aircraft were donated to museums.

86 | POLISH AVIATION MUSEUM CRACOW

Ilyushin Il-28R/S-Il-28

In 1948 the Ilyushin Design Bureau developed a twin jet engine bomber aircraft, the Il-28. The prototype was powered by two Rolls-Royce Nene engines, later replaced by their Soviet clone the RD-45. An improved version powered by two VK-1 engines, with engine nacelles design according to the Area Rule for reaching higher speed, entered production in 1949. It was fitted with a Soviet copy of the famous Norden bombsight. Combat units received their first aircraft in 1950. Also in 1950 a reconnaissance version, the Il-28R, with bomb bay adapted to carry cameras, light markers and additional fuel tanks, made its first flight. Later some Il-28Rs were converted for ECM duties by installation of specialized equipment. A nuclear weapon carrier and a torpedo bomber version for naval aviation were also built.

Poland purchased 80 aircraft, bomber and reconnaissance versions. Some were converted to the ECM version. They were used between 1952 and 1977.

PZL TS-11 *Iskra*

Two-seat jet trainer designed in 1958 by a team supervised by Tadeusz Sołtyk. The prototype first flew 1960 with a British Bristol-Siddeley Viper 8 engine, because of problems with intended SO-1 engine, which was being designed simultaneously. The aircraft, named *Iskra* (Spark) has proved to be very successful. In 1961 the *Iskra* took part in a contest for a jet trainer for the air forces of the Warsaw Pact member countries, held in the Soviet Union. Its rivals were the Soviet Yak-30 and Czechoslovak Aero L-29 *Delfin*. For political and other reasons the L-29 was the winner, but Poland stayed with the *Iskra*, having commenced series production in WSK PZL Mielec. Because of constant problems with the SO-1 engine, WSK PZL Rzeszów commenced production of the HO-10 engine, based on the B-S Viper. The Iskra *bis* A version entered service in 1964. In 1966 an Iskra *bis* B version was designed, with upgraded avionics and underwing armament pylons. In 1972 a reconnaissance and artillery spotting version, the *Iskra* 200 was designed, which was produced as Iskra *bis* C. Also in 1972 a single-seat strike version the *Iskra* 200BR was designed, but did not enter production. In 1973 the *Iskra* 200SB was designed, which was produced as Iskra *bis* D. In 1975 production of a training and reconnaissance version, the Iskra *bis* DF, commenced.

In 1964 the *Iskra* set four world speed records for this class of aircraft.

In 1975 the Indian Air Force purchased 50 *Iskra bis* D aircraft. Production finally ceased in 1987. A total of 427 aircraft was built. In the Polish Air Force *Iskra*s are still used for advanced training and as aerobatic aircraft by a military display team, the "White & Red Sparks". Naval Aviation used to employ the *Iskra* for maritime reconnaissance.

POLISH AVIATION MUSEUM CRACOW

Sukhoi Su-7BM

Su-7 is a supersonic fighter-bomber aircraft, designed to meet requirements for a new frontline fighter issued by the USSR in 1953. The MiG-21 won the contest and the Su-7 was used as a base to design a tactical fighter-bomber, capable of carrying a nuclear weapon, equivalent to new American F-100 C/D Super Sabre and F-105 Thunderchief aircraft. The prototype of the Su-7B first flew in 1959 and entered service in 1961 to become the main strike force of Soviet Air Force tactical units for a long time. In 1962 the Su-7BM version, with upgraded engine and avionics and range extended by external fuel tanks, was developed.

In 1964 the Polish Air Force purchased 6 Su-7BM aircraft assigned to carrying nuclear weapon, to enhance Warsaw Pact offensive capabilities in case of war.

Sukhoi Su-7BKL

In 1963 a new version of the Su-7BM was designed, with upgraded engine, increased fuel capacity, new double canopy brake chute system with an upper container, landing gear with skids enabling operations from unpaved airstrips, jettisonable rocket boosters, new KS-4 ejection seat, and bomb load increased to 2,500 kg. This version was designated Su-7BKL. It entered production in 1965, replacing the Su-7BM. The Polish Air Force purchased 30 aircraft, delivered between 1966 and 1972.

The Su-7 had several drawbacks, like high fuel consumption, high approach and landing speeds and restricted cockpit visibility, which hampered attacking ground targets with conventional weapons. The Polish Air Force purchased 30 aircraft, delivered between 1966 and 1972.

90 | POLISH AVIATION MUSEUM CRACOW

Sukhoi Su-7U

Two-seat trainer version of the Su-7, used for type conversion. The prototype was built and first flew in 1965. The construction was based on the Su-7BM airframe, but had several modifications implemented in the Su-7BKL, like the under-fin brake chute container and rocket boosters. The fuselage was lengthened by 8 in to accommodate the aft cockpit. The trainee and instructor occupied two separate pressurized cockpits in tandem. Increased weight of the two-seat aircraft caused a reduction of fuel capacity and bomb load.

The Polish Air Force purchased 8 aircraft, delivered 1969-1984. All versions of the Su-7 stayed in service in Poland until the early 1990s.

Sukhoi Su-20

In 1960s in the USSR research on improving the flight characteristics of the Su-7 was conducted. Many problems of this aircraft, such as long take-off and landing run caused by high lift-off and touchdown speeds, and poor manoeuvrability, could be solved by variable wing geometry. In 1965 a new aircraft with a variable geometry wing, based on the Su-7, was designed. First flight took place in 1966 and in 1967 the aircraft, designated Su-17, entered production and service. It was equipped with new navigation and fire control systems, but short range, caused by the uneconomical AL-7 engine, was still a problem. In 1972 a new, upgraded version, the Su-17M with modern AL-21 engine based on the American J-79, was developed. The new aircraft had increased fuel capacity, redesigned fuselage, refined wing sweep gear, weapons load increased to 8,000 lb and guided missile capability. It remained in production until 1976. In 1972 an export version, the Su-20, capable of carrying R-3S and R-13M air-to-air missiles, was designed.

The Polish Air Force purchased 26 aircraft, delivered 1974-1977, being the sole operator of the Su-20 among Warsaw Pact member countries. They were operated by 7th Bomber & Reconnaissance Regiment at Powidz. The Su-20 was the first type of aircraft with variable geometry operated by the Polish Air Force. Some aircraft were fitted with a camera mounted behind the nosewheel well, thus they were unofficially designated Su-20R. The Su-20s remained in service in Poland until 1997. The successor of the Su-20 is the Su-22, which is still the main attack aircraft of the Polish Air Force.

92 | POLISH AVIATION MUSEUM CRACOW

Sukhoi Su-22

Su-22 is a fighter-bomber aircraft featuring variable wing geometry, which is a further development of the Su-17 (export designation Su-20), fitted with upgraded navigation and targeting equipment. The Su-17M4 (export designation Su-22M4) was the most advanced version, in production since 1980, featuring the PrNK-54 navigation and targeting system, enabling automatic target approach and dropping ordnance without visual contact, and the Klon laser target indicator for laser guided missiles.

Poland purchased 100 aircraft, delivered between 1984 and 1985. A number of them, after overhauls and upgrades, are still operated by the Polish Air Force as the main type of strike aircraft.

Sukhoi Su-22UM3K is a two-seat combat trainer variant of the Su-22, used for type conversion and training, based on the older Su-22M3. Despite reduced armament the aircraft retains significant combat capabilities.

Republic F-84F Thunderstreak

Republic F-84F Thunderstreak is an American fighter-bomber aircraft, which in the 1950s was the main strike aircraft of many NATO countries. It was developed as an upgraded version of the F-84E Thunderjet with swept wings. The prototype, designated YF-96A, first flew on 3rd June 1950. Test flights proved that a new, more powerful engine was necessary. The British Bristol-Siddeley Sapphire, built in the USA as the Curtiss YJ-65-W-1, was chosen. The outbreak of the Korean War revealed the need for new strike aircraft, capable of carrying tactical nuclear weapon. The designation was changed to F-84F to obtain Congress funding more easily for development of an existing design rather than a totally new one. The development was plagued with many engine and airframe problems which led to a temporary solution in the form of an upgraded F-84G straight wing version, which happened to be the version built in the largest numbers, with production exceeding 3,000. The first production F-84Fs entered service in the USAF as late as 1954. Up to 1957 a total of 2348 were built , 2111 by the Republic plant at Farmingdale and 237 by General Motors at Kansas City. Some USAF aircraft were capable of carrying the Mark 7 tactical nuclear bomb on a special pylon on the inner port hard point. The RF-84F Thunderflash photo reconnaissance version, with air intakes in the wing roots and cameras in the nose, was also developed.

In the USAF the F-84F's service was rather short, because of the long birth process and before the end of the decade it was replaced by aircraft with more advanced equipment and higher performance, like the F-100 Super Sabre and F-101 Voodoo. By 1958 all ex-USAF were transferred to Air National Guard units, from which the last ones were retired in 1972. The USAF's aerobatic display team, the Thunderbirds, flew F-84Fs during the 1955 and 1956 seasons. A subsequent fighter-bomber aircraft designed by Republic was the supersonic F-105 Thunderchief, nicknamed Thud, hence the F-84F was nicknamed Thud's mother.

F-84F and RF-84F aircraft were delivered within the Military Assistance Program to European NATO countries. The largest operator was Germany, which operated 450. France purchased 328 aircraft, Belgium 197, the Netherlands 180 and Italy 150. In the early 1960s the F-84Fs were replaced by the supersonic F-104G Starfighter. Subsequent operators were Turkey, which obtained 125 aircraft from Germany and the Netherlands, and Greece, which obtained 91. The last F-84Fs were retired by the Turkish Air Force in 1982. In 1991 the Hellenic Air Force retired their last three RF-84Fs and this was the end of the service life of the F-84 family.

The only country which used the F-84F and RF-84F in combat was France. During the Suez Crisis in October 1956 France sent to the theatre two squadrons, which operated from the Lydda base in Israel and Akrotiri on Cyprus. Their biggest success was destroying 20 Egyptian Il-28 bombers at a base near Luxor on November 5th. The French lost one aircraft and pilot. The F-84F took also part in Turkish-Greek clashes over Cyprus, but no information about these operations is available.

The displayed aircraft, number FU-36, was donated by the Royal Museum of the Armed Forces and of Military History in Brussels.

SAAB J35J *Draken*

The SAAB J35J *Draken* is a single-seat fighter built in Sweden, the first of a series of Swedish supersonic combat aircraft. Its successors are the JA37 *Viggen* and JAS39 *Gripen*.

In 1947 in Sweden studies on supersonic fighters, supervised by Eng. Erik Bratt, began. In 1949 technical and tactical specifications of the new fighter were issued in cooperation with Swedish Air Force command. The specifications assumed supersonic speed, high rate of climb, all-weather operational capability, armament consisting of cannons and guided missiles, ability to operate from public roads, easy maintenance and small dimensions to ease transportation and storage. In 1951 the innovatory double delta configuration was adopted. The prototype of the J35 *Draken* (Dragon) first flew in 1955. It was powered by a Rolls-Royce Avon 200 engine, produced under licence by Volvo Flygmotor as the RM6. In 1958 production of the J35A version began. This version was not fully combat capable, due to its reduced avionics equipment. In 1959 a full combat capable version, the J35B, and the two seat training Sk-35C, made their first flights. The J35B was incorporated in the Swedish automatic aerial defense system STRIL 60. In 1960 an upgraded version, the J35D, and in 1963 a reconnaissance version S35E, were designed and entered production. In 1965 the J35F entered service, with a new fire control system, extended external weapons load, capability of carrying new AIM-4C and AIM-26B guided missiles (licence-built in Sweden as RB 28 and RB 27). It remained in production until 1977. Between 1987 and 1991 66 J35F aircraft underwent overhaul and avionics upgrade to adapt them to new AIM-9L Sidewinder guided missiles. They were redesignated J35J. A total of 615 *Drakens* of all versions were built. The *Draken* was exported to Denmark, Finland and Austria. In Austria they are still in service.

The displayed aircraft, donated by the Swedish Air Force, was flown to Cracow in 1998.

SAAB AJSF 37 *Viggen*

The AJSF37 is a reconnaissance variant of the SAAB AJ37 *Viggen*, (the thunderbolt, launched by the Norse god of war Thor), which was the successor to the J32 *Lansen* and J35 *Draken*. Different versions of the *Viggen* were the main combat aircraft of the Swedish Air Force for 30 years. The prototype first flew in 1967. In 1970 an attack-fighter version, the AJ37, entered production and subsequently a two-seat training version, the Sk37, in 1972. Maritime patrol and reconnaissance version SH37, a photo reconnaissance version SF37 and a fighter version JA37 were subsequently developed. A total of 329 aircraft of all versions were built. Between 1992 and 1998 25 SF37 aircraft were upgraded to AJSF37 standard. Modifications included a computer mission planning system and ability to carry four AIM-9L/M missiles. Main equipment consists of six Matra cameras – three SKa-24-120, one nose and two oblique mounted for horizon-to-horizon coverage, a wide angle SKa-24-57 and two SKa-24-600 for high altitude pictures under the nose. The aircraft could also carry active and passive ECM pods.

The displayed aircraft, number 37 954, was built in 1977 as the fifth of 28 SF37s. With tactical number 54 it served with *Flygflottij* 21 (21st Wing) at Lulea–Kallax, the northernmost Swedish military air base, near the Arctic Circle. It was donated by the Swedish Air Force and flown to Cracow in November 2005.

CHAPTER 3: THE OPEN AIR EXHIBITION AND MIG ALLEY

Northrop F-5E Tiger II

In the 1950s Northrop designed a lightweight fighter/attack aircraft, the N-156, in a combat single-seat F and two-seat training T versions, powered by two new GE J85 engines. Fuselage design was according to the Area Rule. In 1961 a trainer version named T-38 Talon entered service, being one of only a few supersonic trainers. N-156F prototype first flew in 1959 and entered production in 1963 as the F-5A "Freedom Fighter". Due to its simple construction and reasonable price the F-5 was included in the Military Assistance Program for US allies. It was built in several versions, also under licence in Canada, Taiwan, Netherlands and Spain.

The F-5E Tiger II version, with extended wingspan and upgraded avionics giving better air-to air combat capabilities, first flew in 1972. The F-5E won the International Fighter Aircraft contest for a fighter for countries threatened by a conflict with opponents operating late versions of MiG-21. It was exported to many countries, e.g. Iran and South Vietnam, where they took part in the war. Some were captured by the North Vietnamese army after the armistice in 1975. To date F-5Es have been operated by many countries, e.g. Switzerland. The F-5 was one of most successful export products of the US aviation industry.

In the USA the F-5s were used by the Aggressor training squadrons, simulating the MiG-21 in practice aerial combats. The F-5 starred in the famous "Top Gun" movie, playing fictional "MiG-28" Russian fighters.

The displayed aircraft served in the South Vietnam Air Force. In 1975 it was captured by North Vietnamese troops and sent to Poland for technical research at the Polish Air Force Technical Institute, where it was stripped of many important parts.

POLISH AVIATION MUSEUM CRACOW | 97

Cessna A-37B Dragonfly

The experience gained on operations against guerilla units in Asian and African countries during the early 1960s showed that a new lightweight attack aircraft for counterinsurgency (COIN) operations was needed. In 1963 in the USA a prototype of the Cessna YAT-37D strike aircraft, based on the T-37 "Tweet" trainer, was designed. It had new, more powerful J85 engines, fixed machine gun, armoured cockpit, strengthened fuselage construction, wingtip tanks and 6 underwing pylons for armament and additional tanks. In 1967 39 aircraft, named A-37A Dragonfly, were built. 25 aircraft were assigned to the 640th Air Commando Squadron at Bien Hoa Air Base in Vietnam for combat use evaluation (operation Combat Dragon). Based on the results, an improved version, the A-37B with more powerful J85-GE-17 engines, flight refuelling system and upgraded avionics was developed. 577 aircraft were built, 254 were provided to South Vietnamese Air Force. Most of them were captured by the North Vietnamese army after the defeat of South Vietnamese forces in 1975. They were incorporated by the North Vietnamese Air Force and took part in the war in Cambodia. 169 aircraft were provided by the US within the Military Assistance Program to South American countries, where they took part in several local conflicts. In the USA after the Vietnam War the Dragonflies were assigned to Air National Guard units. 130 aircraft were modified to Forward Air Control OA-37s. They were retired from service in the mid 1990s

The displayed aircraft was sent during the 1970s from Vietnam to Poland for technical research at the Polish Air Force Technical Institute, where it was stripped of many important parts.

LOCKHEED F-104S STARFIGHTER

Lockheed F-104 Starfighter was designed in the early 1950s by Clarence "Kelly" Johnson, basing on experience gained by the USAF during the Korean War. American fighter pilots who fought in Korea wanted a simple, lightweight fighter with high performance and manoeuverability. Later the conception changed and due to the development of guided air-to-air missiles manoeuverability was sacrificed for speed. So the F-104 Starfighter, an unusual aircraft, far ahead of its time, was developed. A sleek fuselage ended with the long needle of the pitot tube and housing the powerful GE J79 engine, the T-shaped tailplane and tiny trapezoid wings with very sharp leading edges caused the Starfighter to be nicknamed "a missile with a man in it".

In the USAF its service as an air defense fighter was rather short and insignificant, however it included two deployments to Vietnam during 1965 and 1966–1967, during which four aircraft were lost – one was shot down by Vietnamese anti-aircraft defenses, one by Chinese fighters over the Hainan island and two were lost in a mid–air collision.

The oldest variant of the Starfighter, the F-104A, was operated by Jordan, Taiwan and Pakistan. The Pakistani Starfighters scored five kills over Indian aircraft during the Pakistani – Indian conflict in December 1971.

In the 1960s the Starfighter became the main type of nuclear-capable strike fighter and reconnaissance aircraft in some European NATO member countries: Germany, Netherlands, Belgium, Spain, Greece, Italy, Turkey, Denmark and Norway. The export version, with enhanced air-to-ground capabilities, was designated F-104G (G for Germany, which was the first customer). It was also operated by Canada and Japan. It was licence built by MBB in Germany, Fokker in the Netherlands, SABCA in Belgium, Fiat in Italy, Canadair in Canada and Mitsubishi in Japan.

Italy was the country which operated the Starfighter for the longest time. The Fiat company undertook licence production of the F-104G in 1962. 125 aircraft were built. In 1965 the first unit became operational. As Italy operated the Starfighters mainly in the fighter interceptor role, during 1965–66 a new version, the F-104S with upgraded engine and avionics, capable of carrying AIM-7 Sparrow radar-guided missiles, was developed. Deliveries of this version, in fighter-bomber and interceptor roles, lasted from 1969 until 1979. 246 aircraft were built, including 40 for Turkey.

In late 1980s the majority of Italian F-104S underwent the ASA avionics upgrade, enabling the aircraft to carry the Aspide 1A missile, an Italian upgraded version of the Sparrow, and the new version of the Sidewinder, the AIM-9L. In 1990s the Italian Air Force was planning to replace Starfighters with the Eurofighter Typhoon, but the delay of the Eurofighter program resulted in the necessity of another avionics upgrade, designated ASA-M, within which communication and navigation instruments from the AMX aircraft were installed.

The displayed aircraft, number MM 6876, was donated by the Italian Air Force in November 2008 for the exhibition on the 60th anniversary of NATO. It served with the 9th Fighter Wing (9o *Stormo*) "Francesco Baracca" at Grazzanise near Naples. During its service it underwent both avionics upgrades.

Dassault Mirage 5BA

The Mirage 5BA is a fighter-bomber developed by the Dassault company in France. The aircraft was built for the French Air Force and foreign customers. The -BA variant was built for the Belgian Air Force. The first letter in the variant designation indicated the customer country.

The Mirage 5 was a development of the Mirage III fighter, featuring the characteristic Delta wing layout. The Mirage 5 was developed in the second half of the 1960s, as a response to an Israeli order for a fighter-bomber aircraft. The design was based on the Mirage III, but featured simplified avionics without radar.

The prototype first flew in 1967. The embargo on armaments to Israel, declared by the French government after the Six Day War in 1967, caused the first aircraft, built initially for Israel in 1970, to be taken over by the French Air Force.

The Mirage 5 was built in three variants – fighter-bomber, reconnaissance and two-seat combat trainer. Most of 400 aircraft built were sold to foreign customers. Many of them were later upgraded, aerodynamic improvements as well as new targeting and navigation systems were introduced.

The displayed aircraft is a Mirage 5BA (fighter-bomber), number BA 03, one of 63 operated by Belgium, which, apart from Libya, was the largest operator of the type. Apart from these, Belgium also operated 27 aircraft of the reconnaissance variant (BR) and 16 combat trainers (BD). The aircraft was built in 1970 by the SABCA plant at Gosselies and served with the Belgian Air Force until 1991. It was donated by the Royal Museum of the Armed Forces and of Military History in May 2008 for the exhibition on the 60th anniversary of NATO. The aircraft was exchanged for a Mi-2 helicopter.

The Mirage III and V were amongst the best combat aircraft of the 1950s and 1960s. They combined modern aerodynamics with superb performance and manoeuverability. They were formidable in air combat and became one of the greatest export hits of the French aviation industry.

Ling Temco Vought A-7P Corsair II

The LTV A-7 Corsair II is an American attack aircraft, designed in the 1960s for the US Navy as the successor of the Douglas A-4 Skyhawk. The design was based on the Vought F-8 Crusader fighter. The Corsair II was a simplified, subsonic version of the Crusader. The name Corsair was inherited from the famous and formidable Vought F4U Corsair attack aircraft from the Second World War, used also in the Korean War. The prototype first flew on September 27th, 1965 and in late 1966 the first production aircraft of the A-7A version entered service. Initially the A-7A and A-7B versions for the US Navy, armed with two 20 mm Colt Mk12 cannons and powered by Pratt&Whitney TF-30 turbofans, were developed. The ordnance load exceeded 6 tons. In December 1967 the first A-7A unit, VA-147 "Argonauts", went in action in Vietnam, where the Corsair II proved to be very effective in combat. The US Air Force showed interest in the aircraft and ordered the A-7D version, with more powerful Allison TF-41 engine (licence-built version of the Rolls-Royce Spey), upgraded avionics, M61 Vulcan cannon and flying boom aerial refuelling receptacle. Subsequent versions for US Navy were the A-7C and the ultimate A-7E, a carrier-based derivative of the A-7D. Production continued until 1984 and 1,589 aircraft of all versions were built. The A-7 took part in the Vietnam War, the invasion of Grenada and the war in Lebanon in 1983, the retaliatory attack on Libya in 1986 and the Desert Storm operation in Iraq in 1991. After Desert Storm the last A-7Es were retired from US Navy, superseded by the F/A-18C Hornet.

Apart from the US, A-7s were operated by Portugal, Greece and Thailand. In the early 1980s the Portuguese Air Force purchased 50 A-7P aircraft, the A-7A with TF-30-408 engine from the A-7C and avionics from the A-7E. Portugal operated these aircraft until 1999. The displayed aircraft was exchanged for a MiG-21PFM with the Portuguese Air Force Museum.

Lisunov Li-2

In the mid 1930s in the USA the Douglas DC-3 was designed. It became one of the world's most successful and popular passenger/transport aircraft. Its military version, C-47 Skytrain (in British nomenclature "Dakota"), was the main type of transport aircraft used by the Allies during World War Two.

In 1938 the USSR purchased a licence for the DC-3. Several modifications adapting the aircraft to service in the USSR, including structure strengthening, replacing the main entry door and change of engines, were applied by the design team of Boris Lisunov. The aircraft entered production in 1939 as the PS-84. In 1941 the designation was changed to Li-2. Production continued until 1947. Some 3,000 aircraft were built.

The Li-2 was produced in transport, passenger, aerial photography, bomber, long range and high altitude versions. During WW II they conducted airlift tasks over the Eastern Front. In 1943 paratroopers from the Polish Special Duties Battalion were dropped from Li-2 troop carriers.

After the war Li-2s were operated by Polish Airlines LOT until 1969 and by the air force as transport aircraft until 1974. Air Traffic and Airport Administration used one aircraft for navigation aids calibration.

The displayed aircraft was built in 1943. During the war it was operated by the Soviet air force. After the war it was delivered to the Polish Air Force. From 1950-1974 it served at the Officer Flying School in Dęblin.

Chapter 3: The open air exhibition and MiG Alley

POLISH AVIATION MUSEUM CRACOW | 103

Ilyushin (VEB) Il-14S

In 1945 in the USSR the Ilyushin Il-12 passenger aircraft, designed to replace Li-2 and DC-3, made its first flight. It entered production in 1948. In 1950 an upgraded version, the Il-14 with more powerful and economical engines, redesigned wings and vertical fin, made its first flight. Initially the 18-seat Il-14P was produced. In 1956 a new version with lengthened fuselage, seating up to 32 passengers, was developed. Cargo versions, designated Il-14G or Il-14T and a paratroop carrier version Il-14D were also designed. 3,500 aircraft were built. 80 Il-14P were licence-built in East Germany and 200 aircraft were built in Czechoslovakia, under the designation Avia Av-14.

Il-14 were used in air transport in the USSR and socialist countries. In Poland the Il-14 was operated by Polish Airlines LOT until 1974 and by military aviation until the early '90s. Air Traffic and Airport Administration used one aircraft for navigation aids calibration.

The displayed aircraft was built in 1959 in East Germany as an executive transport. It was operated by the 36th Special Air Transport Regiment for VIP transport. It was often used by Władysław Gomułka, the First Secretary of the Polish United Labour Party. It was retired from service in 1987 and donated to the museum.

Yakovlev Yak-40

The Yak-40 was designed in 1966 by the Yakovlev design bureau as a regional passenger aircraft. It is adapted for operating from short, unpaved airstrips, and for that purpose has long unswept wings and landing gear with wheels of large diameter. The passenger version carries 32 passengers. Many specialized versions and executive VIP transports were also developed. The first Yak-40s were delivered to Poland in 1973 and since then they have been used for VIP transport by the 36th Special Air Transport Regiment. A target tug version for gunnery practice was also developed in Poland. In the late 1980s Polish Airlines LOT operated Yak-40s leased from the 36th Wing.

The displayed aircraft, number 037, was operated by 36th Special Air Transport Regiment until 2003. In 2006 it was donated to the Museum.

SEPECAT Jaguar GR.1

The Jaguar is an attack aircraft designed during the 1960s by an Anglo-French consortium, responding for a demand by the French and Royal Air Forces for a supersonic trainer and light attack aircraft. The French Air Force were seeking an attack aircraft to replace the F-84F Thunderstreak, F-100 Super Sabre and Dassault *Mystere* B.2 and a trainer to replace the Lockheed T-33 and Fouga Magister. The RAF was seeking a successor for the Folland Gnat and Hawker Hunter T.7 advanced trainers. Due to similar requirements both countries decided on cooperation, establishing the SEPECAT (*Société Européenne de Production de l'Avion d'École de Combat et d'Appui Tactique*, European Company for Production of Combat Trainer and Tactical Support Aircraft) consortium in 1966. It was the second such Anglo-French enterprise at that time (the first was the Concorde supersonic passenger aircraft). The design, using the area rule, was based on French Breguet Br.121. The Rolls-Royce and Turbomeca companies undertook joint studies on the Adour engine intended for the new aircraft, which was named Jaguar, with approval of the famous British car manufacturer. France and Great Britain had different requirements, so versions built for each country differed in respect of equipment and armament. The French aircraft were armed with two 30 mm DEFA cannon, while the British aircraft were armed with two Aden cannon of the same calibre. The French Air Force intended to use the aircraft in former African colonies, while the RAF aircraft were supposed to take part in fending off potential invasion by the Warsaw Pact forces of NATO countries, thus it featured much more complex avionics than the French ones, like the Laser Rangefinder & Marked Target Seeker (LRMTS) mounted in the nose. Trainer aircraft built for France were designated Jaguar E, and combat versions Jaguar A. The French also conducted trials with the Jaguar M carrier-based variant, but the results were not satisfactory and studies on the maritime version of the Jaguar were discontinued in favour of the Dassault Super Etendard. British single-seat aircraft were designated Jaguar S, and two seaters Jaguar B. The prototype first flew in 1968. Series production began in 1972 – the French version at Toulouse and the British version at Warton. In the wake of the fuel crisis after the Yom Kippur war in 1973 the interest in the trainer version declined, and the stress on production of the combat version grew. 160 aircraft of the combat version and 40 of the trainer version were built for France and 165 combat aircraft (whose designation was altered to GR.1) and 38 of the trainer version (whose designation was altered to T.2) for Great Britain. The powerplant of the Jaguar GR.1 comprised two Rolls-Royce/Turbomeca Adour 104 turbofan engines rated at 35.75 kN

Up to 4,540 kg (10,000 lb) of ordnance (bombs, rocket launchers, guided missiles, reconnaissance pods or additional fuel tanks) could be carried on four underwing and one ventral pylon. Aircraft of both countries were capable of carrying nuclear weapons.

Initially the Jaguar was not intended for export. France lost interest in developing the design when the Breguet company was bought by Dassault, which commenced production of its own surprisingly similar Mirage F.1 design. The British went on with selling the Jaguar International version on foreign markets. Jaguars were also purchased by India, Ecuador, Oman and Nigeria.

The combat debut of the French Jaguars occurred in 1977 during the stabilization mission in Mauretania. Subsequently the French aircraft were used several times against rebels supported by Libya in Chad. The RAF Jaguars, based in the UK and West Germany, were a vital element of NATO forces in Europe. British and French aircraft took part in Operation Desert Storm in Iraq in 1991 and stabilisation missions over former Yugoslavia in the 1990s. The French Air Force retired the Jaguar in 2001. British aircraft underwent several upgrades (after which they were designated GR.1A and subsequently GR.3) and remained in service until 2007.

The displayed aircraft, serial number XX730, was built in 1974 and served with 6 Squadron RAF until 1985, and subsequently was used for ground instruction at the Defence College of Aeronautical Engineering (DCAE) at Cosford, and was donated to the Museum in February 2010.

Fouga CM.170 *Magister*

The French Fouga CM.170 *Magister* is the world's second purpose-built jet trainer aircraft, intended for training future combat jet pilots. The first was the Dutch Fokker S.14 *Machtrainer*, which appeared a year earlier, but it was built in much smaller numbers and remained in service for a shorter time. The *Magister*'s design was based on the Fouga CM.8 glider, used for tests with jet engines. In 1948 the Fouga company developed the CM.130 aircraft, powered by two Turbomeca *Palas* engines, which proved to be not powerful enough. The design was changed, adapting the airframe to larger Turbomeca *Marbore* II engines. In December 1950 the French Air Force ordered three prototypes, of which the first made its maiden flight in July 1952. In 1954 production of the Fouga CM.170-1 *Magister*, powered by two Turbomeca *Marbore* IIA turbojet engines rated at 3.9 kN (875 lbf) each began. The aircraft could be armed with two 7.5 or 7.62 in machine guns in the nose and up to 140 kg (310 lb) of bombs or rocket missiles on two underwing hardpoints. The aircraft's distinctive features are the V-tail, designed by Polish engineer Jerzy Rudlicki in the early 1930s, and the periscope, providing the instructor with the visibility from the rear cockpit.

The first *Magisters* entered service in the French Air Force in 1956. In 1959 the CM.175 *Zephyr* version, capable of carrier operations and designed for French naval aviation, entered service. 30 aircraft were built. The aircraft's designation changed several times due to industrial mergers – in 1958 the Fouga company was bought by Potez, then by Sud Aviation in 1967 and ultimately by Aerospatiale. In 1960 an upgraded version, the CM.170-2 *Super Magister*, with more powerful *Marbore* IV engines, entered production. 137 aircraft were built up to 1962.

Being a quite an innovative design, the Fouga *Magister* became an export success. The first foreign operator was West Germany, which purchased 62 aircraft and further 188 were licence-built by Heinkel–Messerschmitt (*Flugzeug Union Süd*). Licence production was also undertaken by Valmet in Finland, which built 62 between 1958-1967 and IAI in Israel, which built 36, designated IAI *Tzukit* (thrush). The *Tzukits* featured underwing weapon hardpoints, providing them with ground attack capability. The other foreign operators were Belgium, Austria, Brazil, Ireland, Algeria, Bangladesh, Cameroon, Cambodia, Gabon, Salvador, Togo, Morocco, Libya, Lebanon and Honduras. Production totalled 929 aircraft of all versions. The direct successor of the *Magister* was the Dassault/Dornier Alpha Jet. Apart from training duties, the Magisters were also operated by *Patrouille de France* and the Belgian Red Devils aerobatic teams. Currently a number of aircraft are flown by private owners throughout the world.

The *Magisters* were used in combat in a few conflicts. The first was the attempted secession of Katanga after Congo had become independent in 1960. The Katangese forces had a few *Magisters*. Israeli Air Force *Tzukits* attacked Jordanian armoured forces during the Six Day War in June 1967. During the Nigerian Civil War in late 1960s the Biafran secessionists operated five aircraft.

Mil Mi-4

Widespread use of helicopters by the Americans during the war in Korea sparked the beginning of studies on a transport helicopter in the USSR in late 1951. The Mil Design Bureau designed the WD-12 helicopter, based on the American Sikorsky S-55, powered by an ASh-82W engine, capable of carrying 12 soldiers or 1600 kg maximum load. The prototype first flew in 1952 and entered production as the Mi-4. Series production machines were capable of carrying 16 soldiers. In 1958 an upgraded version the Mi-4A was developed. From 1952-1966 3,307 machines were built. In China 545 machines designated Z-5 were licence built between 1963 and 1979.

The Polish Air Force operated 17 Mi-4As between 1958 and 1979. The pilots nicknamed the helicopter "Kate", comparing it to a not very pretty, but laborious country maid-off-all-work.

In 1955 an anti-submarine version of the Mi-4 entered service. The export version was designated Mi-4ME (pictured). The helicopter was fitted with a surface observation radar and magnetometer and could carry sonobuoys. Weapons consisted of depth charges stored in a bomb bay mounted in the load compartment.

The Mi-4M proved to be inadequate in the anti-submarine role. High level of noise and vibration reduced efficiency and hampered maintenance of the submarine detection equipment. Maritime operations were extremely dangerous due to the single engine and lack of flotation capability - after ditching the helicopter sank immediately, not providing the crew the possibility of bailing out.

Polish Naval Aviation operated 4 Mi-4ME helicopters.

Mil Mi-8

Mi-8 is a medium transport helicopter, powered by two turboshaft engines, designed in the early 1960s at the Mil Design Bureau in the USSR as the successor to the piston powered Mi-4. The first prototype, powered by a single engine, first flew in 1961. The next prototype, powered by two 1,500 hp TV-2 engines, first flew in 1962. The Mi-8 became one of the world's most popular transport helicopters. Numerous versions, including transport, passenger, executive and rescue were developed as well as many specialized subvariants, like the mine-layer and mine-sweeper and flying command post. More than 9,000 were built and the production of developed versions continues. The Mi-14 amphibian helicopter is based on the Mi-8 design. In the NATO code the Mi-8 is called "Hip".

In 1976 the Mi-17 version (in Russia designated Mi-8M) was developed, powered by more powerful TV-3 engines enhancing the helicopter's performance in hot and high environments. This version was used by the Soviet army during the war in Afghanistan. Externally the Mi-17 differs from the Mi-8 by the shape of the engine cowling, which, apart from TV-3 engines houses also the AI-9 auxiliary power unit, and the tail rotor mounted on the left side of the tail boom.

The Polish military have operated the Mi-8 since 1968 in the transport, rescue, executive and passenger versions, and the Mi-17 since 1987. The Polish Navy has operated the Mi-14 in the PŁ anti submarine warfare version since 1980 and PS rescue version since 1984. Polish Mi-8s and Mi-17s took part in the humanitarian mission in Ethiopia during the 1980s and Polish expeditionary forces mission in Iraq and Afghanistan. Helicopters of the 36th Special Air Transport Regiment were used to carry Pope John Paul II during his visits to Poland. Three Mi-8s are also operated by the Police aviation.

The displayed helicopter is a passenger version, serial number 10620, tail number 620, operated by the 36th Special Air Transport Regiment at Warsaw. It was donated to the Museum in December 2009.

Sud-Aviation SA-3160 *Alouette* III

The world's first production turbine powered helicopter was the five seat SE 3130 *Alouette* II designed by Sud-Est in France, which made its first flight in 1955. The subsequent design was the larger *Alouette* III seating seven instead of five persons and featuring wheels instead of landing skids. The prototype first flew in February 1959. The first version was SE-3160 (SA-316A), powered by the Turbomeca *Artouste* III turboshaft engine, rated at 570 hp, built until 1969, superseded by the SA-316B with strengthened transmission and increased take-off weight and the SA-319B, powered by the Turbomeca *Astazou* XIV engine, rated at 600 hp. More than 1,500 were built, most in the SA-316B version. In many countries, including France, Belgium, Netherlands, Austria and Switzerland they are still in service. Licence production was undertaken by Romania (as the IAR-316B), India (as the HAL Chetak) and Switzerland.

In 1964 the Swiss Air Force purchased its first nine *Alouette* III helicopters in France. The next fifteen were purchased in 1966 and between 1972 and 1974 60 helicopters were built under licence at the F+W Emmen works. In the Swiss Air Force the *Alouette* III helicopters are used for liaison, transport, rescue and basic training duties.

The displayed helicopter, serial number 1079, tail number V-257, was built in 1973 by F+W Emmen. It was donated by the Swiss Air Force.

Bell CH-136 Kiowa

In 1960 the US Army announced a contest for a new, turbine-powered four seat Light Observation Helicopter (LOH). Bell Helicopter Company developed the D-250, designated YHO-4. On this project the Model 206 was based, designated YOH-4A. In 1962 five prototypes for Army tests were built. In 1965 the Hughes OH-6A helicopter was announced the winner. After the rejection by the Army Bell made several improvements and commenced production of the civil version, designated Bell 206A JetRanger, which became the world's most popular light turbine powered helicopter. It was also licence built in Italy as the Agusta Bell AB 206.

Because of Hughes' production problems, in 1967 US Army announced another competition. The Bell company submitted the Model 206A, which won and entered service as the Bell OH-58A Kiowa in 1969. It was powered by one 317 hp Allison T63-A-700 turboshaft engine. The armament could be either one M134 7.62 mm Minigun mounted on the M27 Armament Subsystem, or one M129 40 mm Grenade Launcher mounted on the XM8 Armament Subsystem. In August 1969 the first Kiowas saw combat in Vietnam in Air Cavalry units. 45 helicopters were lost during the Vietnam War.

The Bell OH-58 underwent upgrades during the 1970s and 1980s. Initially the OH-58C version, with more powerful engine and enhanced avionics, was developed. There also was an export version, the OH-58B for the Austrian Army. In 1981 the prototype of the OH-58D version made its maiden flight. The OH-58D features a more powerful engine and new transmission gear, four bladed rotor and Mast Mounted Sight above the rotor, with a gyro-stabilized platform containing a TeleVision System (TVS), a Thermal Imaging System (TIS), and a Laser Range Finder/Designator (LRF/D). The armed version is designated OH-58D Kiowa Warrior. The OH-58Ds cooperate with AH-64 Apaches in hunter-killer teams, indicating targets to destroy.

In 1970 Canadian Armed Forces ordered 74 OH-58As, designated CH-136, to replace Hiller UH-12 Nomad helicopters and Cessna L-19 aircraft in the observation role. They were delivered between 1971 and 1982 and remained in service until 1995, replaced by the Bell CH-146 Griffon, Canadian military version of the Bell 412. Other operators apart from the US and Canada are Austria, Australia, Taiwan and Saudi Arabia.

The displayed helicopter, serial number 71-20920, army number 136255, was donated by the Canadian Armed Forces in 2010.

Tupolev Tu-134A

The Tupolev Tu-104, first flown in 1955, was the first Russian jet passenger aircraft. It was based on the Tu-16 bomber design, with engines mounted in the wing roots. A subsequent model of the same configuration was the Tu-124. The Tupolev bureau received an order to design an aircraft similar to the SE-210 Caravelle, with engines mounted in the tail section to reduce noise and vibration. The prototype Tu-124A was based on Tu-124, with redesigned wings, T-tail and new D-20 engines in rear nacelles. The designation was altered to Tu-134 and the aircraft first flew in 1963. Series production aircraft were powered by D-30 engines. It entered service in 1967. In 1968 the Tu-134, was the first Soviet aircraft to receive an international certificate compatible with British BCAR standards, which eased its export and operations in international airspace. In 1970 the Tu-134A version, with upgraded avionics, fuselage stretched 2.1 m to seat 76 passengers, auxiliary power unit, thrust reversers and improved brakes entered production.

Polish Airlines LOT began their jet age with the purchase of 5 Tu-134 aircraft, delivered between 1968-1969. Between 1973 and 1978 7 Tu-134A aircraft were delivered. They remained in service until the early 1990s. Between 1974 and 1991 the Polish Air Force operated two Tu-134s for VIP transport. Soviet and Russian Air Forces use Tu-134 for transport and several other duties, like bomber pilot, navigator and radar operator training and electronic surveillance. In civil aviation Tu-134s are still operated by several carriers in former USSR countries.

PZL M-15 *Belfegor*

In the early 1970s in the USSR studies on jet powered agricultural aircraft began, in which the Polish aviation industry was also involved. In 1971 at WSK Mielec design work on the M-15 aircraft commenced. The M-15 was a fixed gear biplane, powered by an AI-25 turbofan engine, known from the Yak-40 and the Aero L-39 *Albatros*. The prototype first flew in 1974 and in 1976 series production began.

The aircraft proved to be exceptionally expensive in production and operation. Its use in the USSR was a great disappointment. In 1979 production was cancelled after 175 aircraft were built.

The displayed aircraft is the last *Belfegor* built. It was not collected by the customer and was sent directly from the Mielec plant to the museum.

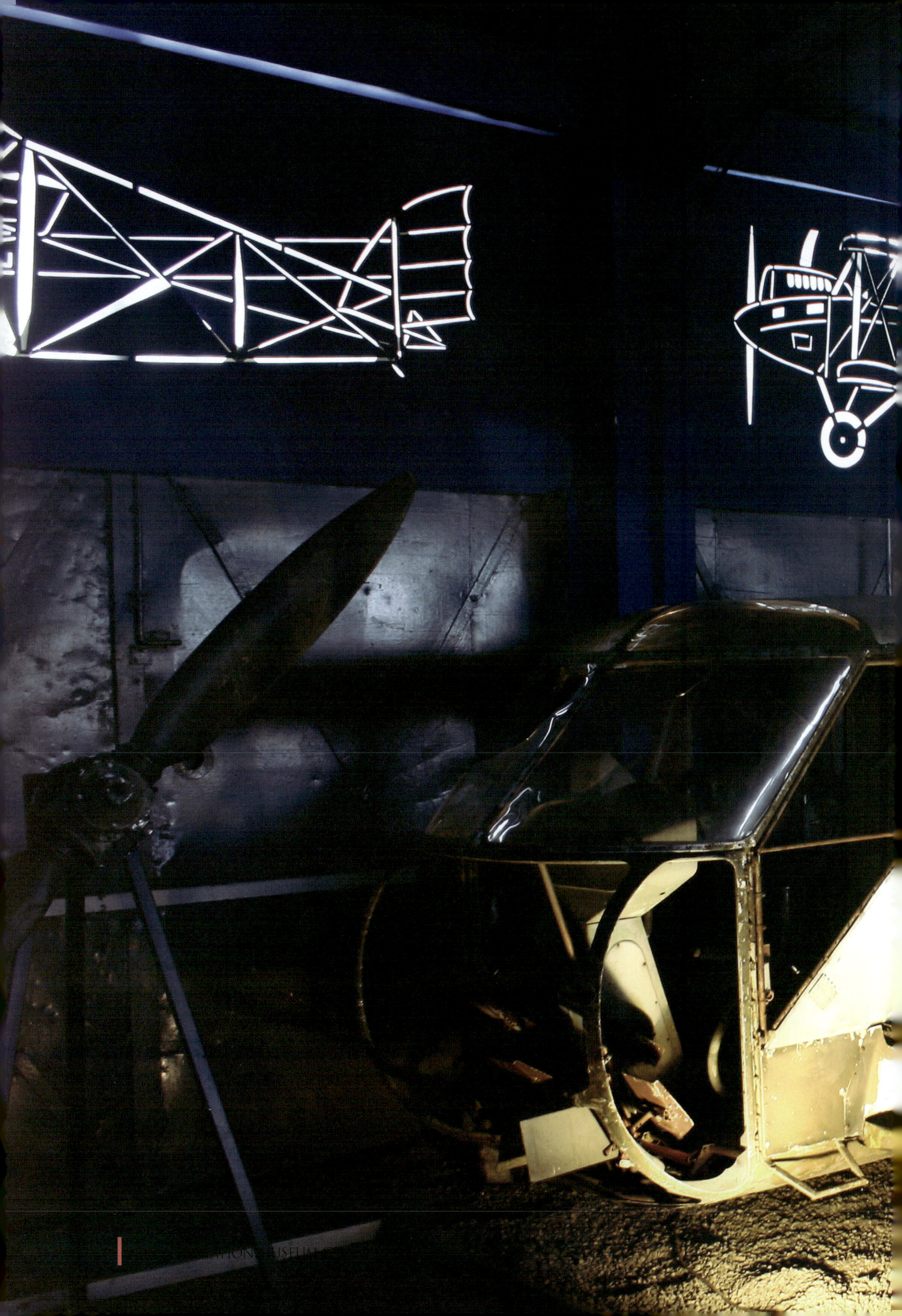

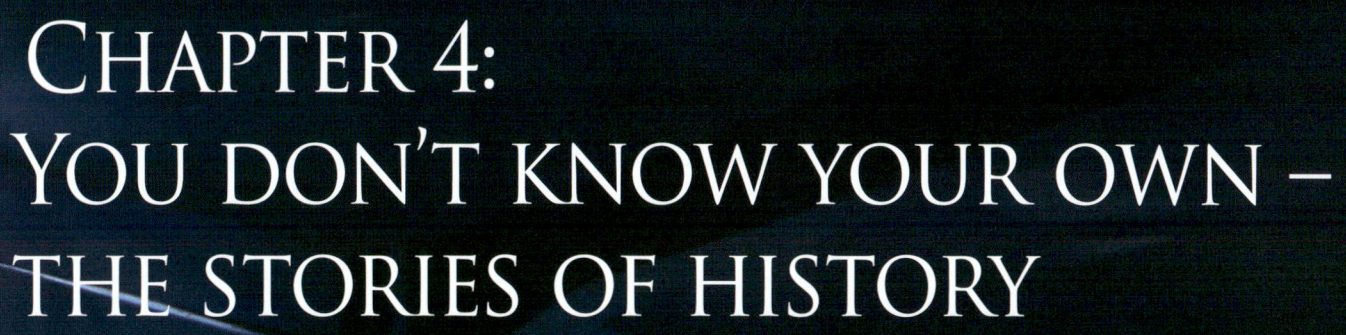

Chapter 4:
You don't know your own – the stories of history

"You don't know your own – the stories of history" is an exhibition which is distinguished by an exceptional atmosphere, at which the oldest aircraft are displayed in original condition, in which they have survived until today. As we enter this exhibition, we move back in time one hundred years, to the beginnings of aviation.

There are two groups of exhibits in this section. The first one comprises aircraft from the pioneer period of aviation (Levavasseur Antoinette, Etrich Taube, Geest Moewe IV, AEG Wagner Eule) and German aircraft built before the Second World War (engine nacelle of the Zeppelin Staaken R.VI giant bomber, used by the Germans to attack London during the First World War, Heinkel He-5f reconnaissance floatplane, two-seat trainer and tourer Albatros L.101, and the fuselage of the Messerschmitt Me 209 V1 which set an air speed record in April 1939).

The second group comprises less known Polish prototype constructions of the post-war period, like the LWD *Szpak* 2, the first aircraft built in Poland after the Second World War, HWL *Pegaz* motoglider, the prototype of liaison aircraft LWD *Żuraw*, BŻ-4 *Żuk* experimental helicopter, designed by Bronisław Żurakowski during the 1950s and the prototype of SZD-27 *Kormoran* metal training glider from the 1960s.

Levavasseur Antoinette

The Levavasseur Antoinette, designed by Leon Levavasseur in 1908, is one of the first aircraft built in Europe. It was powered by an engine designed by Leon Levavasseur, with direct fuel injection and vapour cooling system.

The name Antoinette originates from the name of Levavasseur's daughter. In 1909 a British pilot Hubert Latham made a flight from Paris to Berlin in an Antoinette. The aircraft aroused great interest there, which resulted in the undertaking of licence production by the Albatros company in 1910 and the displayed aircraft belonged to that production batch. Latham also three times attempted to fly in an Antoinette over the English Channel. Although these attempts failed, he managed to reach for the first time an altitude of 1,000 meters in an Antoinette.

The Antoinettes were built in large numbers in various versions, differing between each other by engines, undercarriage types and control systems. In the earlier models roll was controlled by wing warping, later models were fitted with ailerons. The Antoinette IV was featured in a 1965 British comedy movie "Those Magnificent Men in Their Flying Machines".

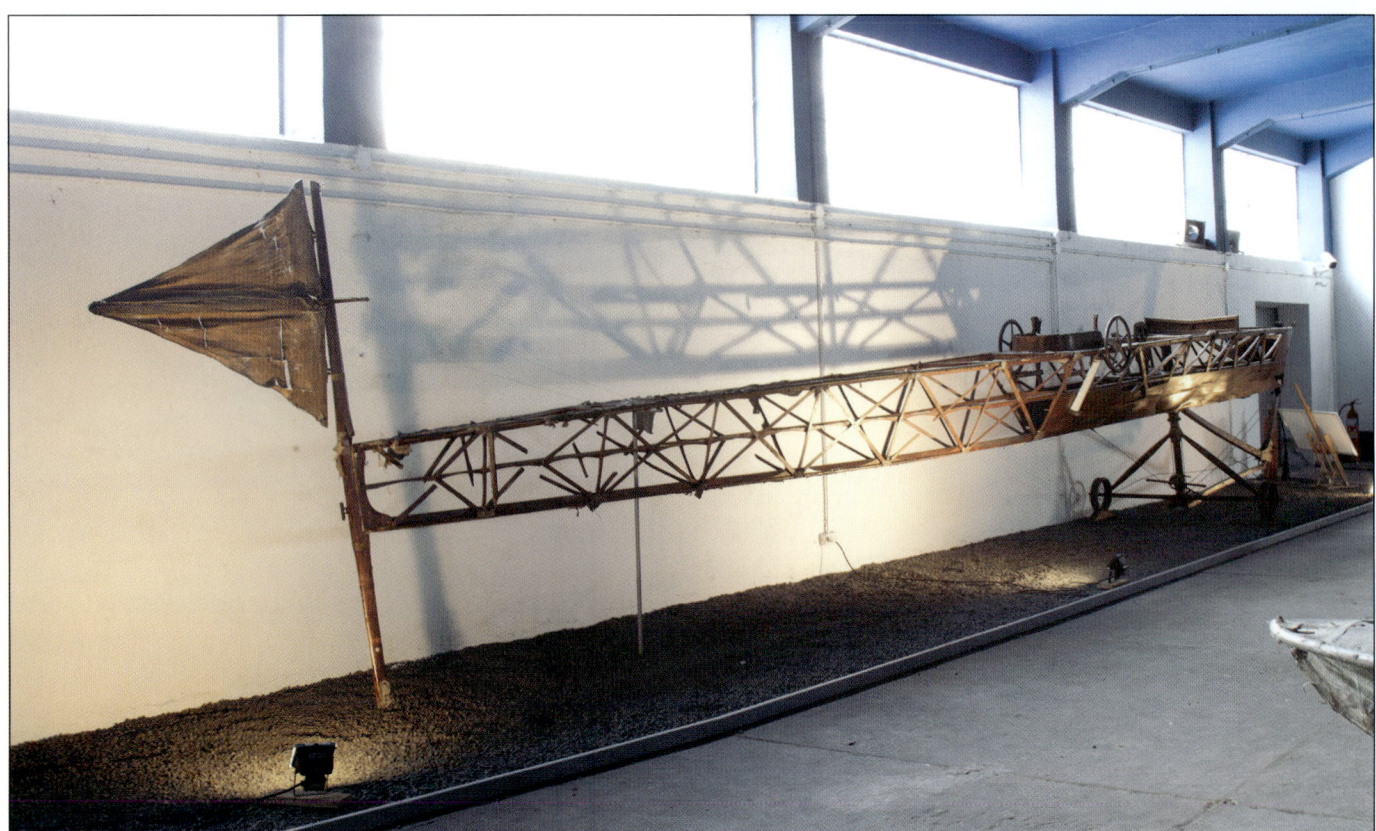

116 | POLISH AVIATION MUSEUM CRACOW

Friedrich Etrich *Taube*

The Friedrich Etrich *Taube* (Pigeon) is one of the best aircraft of the very beginnings of aviation, designed by Igo Etrich in 1910. It had good flying characteristics thanks to which it was used by many aviation pioneers. The *Taube* owes its good flying characteristics to the shape of the wing, resembling the shape of the Zanonia palm seed. The wings feature no ailerons, roll was controlled by warping the wingtips, made of bamboo, as with a bird's wings. The Rumpler company purchased the licence and developed the construction further. The *Taubes* were the first aircraft of Austro-Hungarian aviation, which operated from the Cracow Rakowice airfield. The displayed aircraft is a replica built by Alfred Friedrich in 1936. It was displayed during the Olympic Games in Berlin in 1936.

Heinkel He-5f

One of the most famous German aircraft designers, Ernst Heinkel, established his own aircraft factory at Warnemünde in 1922. The first projects developed there were low-wing civil and military floatplanes, designated He-3 to He-12. Because the Treaty of Versailles forbade the Germans to build military aircraft, they were built at the Svenska Aero AB (SAAB) company at Lidingö near Stockholm.

One of them was the three-seat reconnaissance He-5. These aircraft were built in three versions during 1926–1928. The displayed aircraft, registered as D-OMIP, is the only surviving example of the type.

118 | POLISH AVIATION MUSEUM CRACOW

Messerschmitt Me 209V1

The Messerschmitt Me 209V1 is a German aircraft designed in the late 1930s to set an absolute air speed record. It was powered by a DB 601 ARJ engine rated at 2,300 hp, with partial evaporation of the cooling water. This system caused several problems, the aircraft had other deficiencies and dangerous flying characteristics. There was a competition among the German designers for setting the speed record. The main rival of the Me 209 was the Heinkel He 100V8 in which Hans Dieterle reached a speed of 746 km/h on March 30th, 1939. On April 26th, 1939 Fritz Wendel set a speed record of 755 km/h in the Me 209V1, which for piston powered aircraft was unmatched until 1969, when Darryl G. Greenamyer reached 778 km/h in a modified Grumman F8F-2 Bearcat. For propaganda reasons in the German media the Me 209 was referred to as the Me 109R, a record version of the production fighter. The German Air Ministry (RLM) ordered a fighter version of the Me 209, but these attempts failed.

AEG Wagner *Eule*

AEG Wagner *Eule* (Owl) was the first aircraft design of AEG, developed at the beginning of the First World War. It was a two seat monoplane with wooden wings and fuselage of welded steel tubes covered with fabric, powered by a rotary engine. The first prototype burnt during ground tests. The second prototype (displayed) made a few flights in 1914. The fuselage design was continued in AEG biplanes built during the First World War.

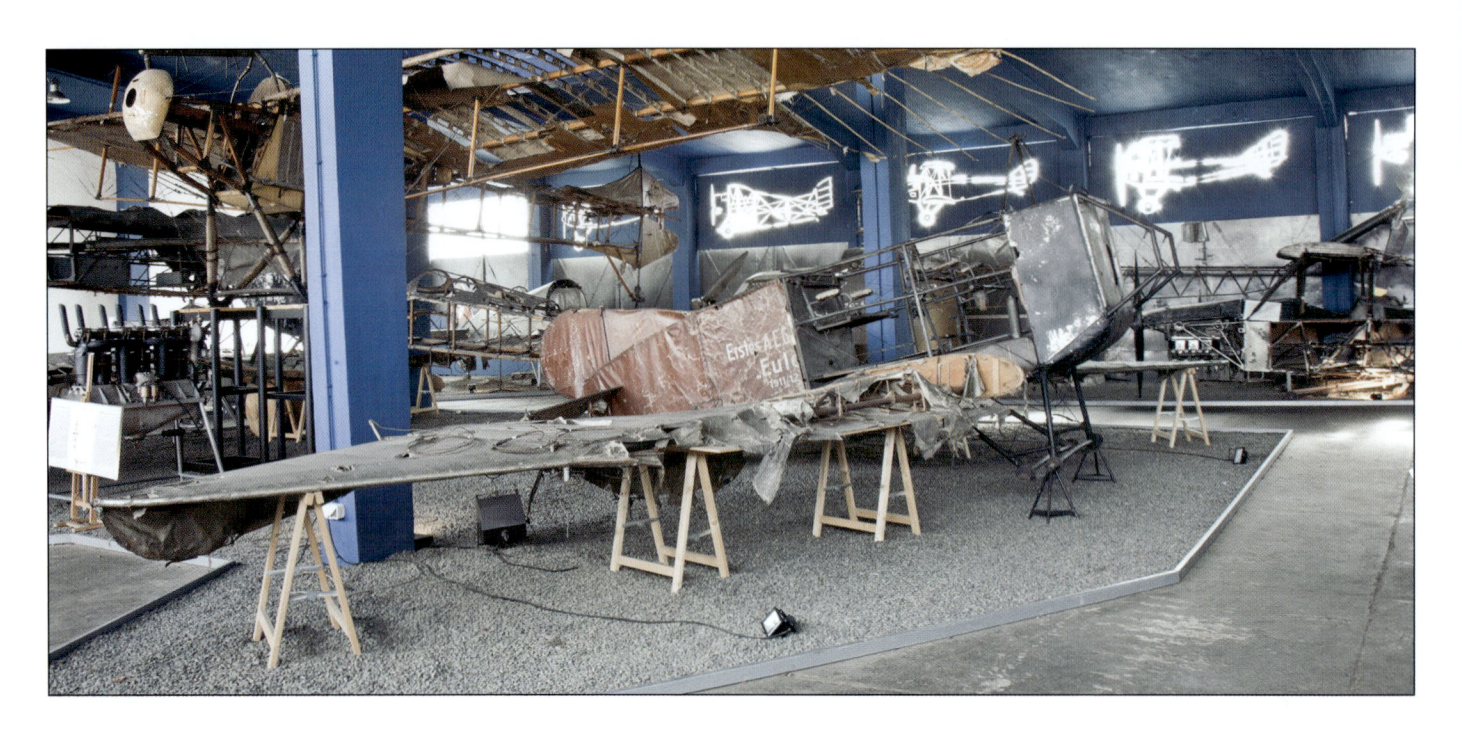

Geest *Moewe* IV

Geest *Moewe* IV, built in 1914, is the only surviving design of German aviation pioneer Waldemar Geest. He patented an arch-shaped wing, in which the anhedral of the tips provided stability. In 1910 he designed a glider whose shape was based on the kittyhawk. From 1911 to 1913 five similar *Moewe* aircraft, numbered I to V, were built.

Albatros L.101

Albatros L.101 is a two-seat German trainer and tourer high wing monoplane of mixed construction, designed at the Albatros company, but produced after Albatros had been taken over by Focke-Wulf in 1932. The prototype took part in the Challenge competition in 1930, but did not complete even the technical trials. 71 aircraft were built by the Berlin division of Focke-Wulf during 1932-1933. They were operated by the German Airline Pilot School as trainers. The displayed aircraft, serial number 245, had the registration D-EKYQ.

LWD *Szpak* 2

LWD *Szpak* 2 (Starling) designed by Tadeusz Sołtyk was the first aircraft built in Poland after the Second World War. Studies on a four seat liaison aircraft began in Lublin in the autumn of 1944. In February 1945, when the Germans were forced back from central Poland, a provisional aircraft factory named Experimental Aircraft Works was established in a furniture factory in Łódź. The prototype *Szpak* 2 (displayed) first flew on October 28th, 1945. The aircraft was used until 1948. In 1947 ten examples of the production *Szpak* 4T were built.

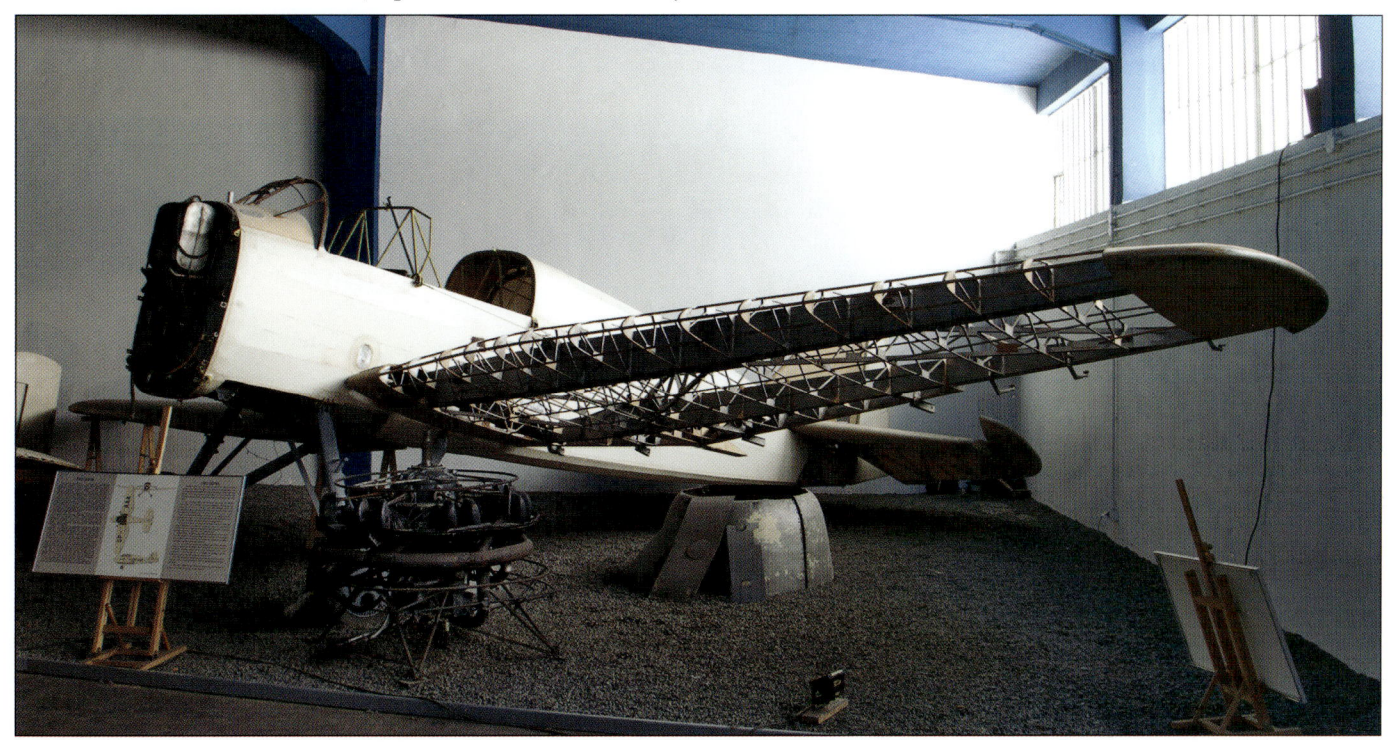

LWD Żuraw

The prototype of the LWD *Żuraw* (Crane) was a military liaison aircraft designed by Tadeusz Sołtyk in the late '40s/early '50s. The maiden flight took place on May 16th, 1951. Three versions, liaison, transport and light bomber were planned, but the aircraft was not a successful design and did not enter production.

BŻ-4 Żuk (Beetle)

BŻ-4 *Żuk* (Beetle) was an experimental helicopter designed by Bronisław Żurakowski. Studies on a four seat helicopter commenced at the Aviation Institute in 1953. The prototype first flew in February 1959. Due to some technical problems and production of the SM-1, the BŻ-4 program was discontinued.

POLISH AVIATION MUSEUM CRACOW

HWL *Pegaz*

HWL *Pegaz* (Pegasus) motoglider was designed by Tadeusz Chyliński in 1945. It was intended mainly to be used by glider pilots for aircraft conversion. A 31 hp Gad horizontally opposed two cylinder engine designed by Stanisław Gajęcki was used as powerplant. Construction of the *Pegaz* was commenced the Scout Air Works in Warsaw in 1948 and completed by the District Air Works. The first flight was on 16th July 1949. The motoglider was operated by the Warsaw Aero Club.

Zeppelin Staaken R.VI bomber

The Zeppelin Staaken R.VI was one of the German *Riesenflugzeuge* (giant aircraft), multi-engine bombers developed during the First World War. The aircraft was a wooden biplane, powered by four engines, two driving pusher and two driving tractor propellers, mounted in two nacelles between the upper and lower wing. Production totalled 13 aircraft, operated by two squadrons RFa 500 and RFa 501 on the eastern front in Kurland, and later from Ghent in Belgium against targets in France and London.

The displayed exhibit is an engine nacelle of aircraft number R.34/16, shot down on 21st April 1918 during a raid on a British airfield at St. Omer, France.

Chapter 5: Engines

124 | POLISH AVIATION MUSEUM CRACOW

CHAPTER 5: ENGINES

Antoinette V-8
France 1908

Le Rhone C
France 1913

V-8 inline engine with vapour cooling system, rated at 60 hp. It was designed by przez Leon Levavasseur. There is a separate injection carburettor for each cylinder. Due to sophisticated construction the engine was not much liked by its users. It powered the Levavasseur Antoinette aircraft. It is the oldest engine in the Museum's collection.

Nine cylinder air cooled rotary engine, rated at 80 hp. It was used in the Nieuport 16, Hanriot HD-14 and Morane-Saulnier MS-30 and MS-35.

Clerget 9B
France 1915

Salmson Z-9
France 1917

Nine cylinder air cooled rotary engine, rated at 130 hp. It was one of the best aircraft engines of the First World War. It was licence built in Great Britain and used in the Nieuport 17, Sopwith Triplane and Sopwith Camel.

Nine cylinder radial engine, rated at 260 hp, with water cooling, which is very unusual for radial engines. It was used in the Salmson 2.

POLISH AVIATION MUSEUM CRACOW | 125

Mercedes E 4 F
Germany 1910

Four-cylinder inline water cooled piston engine, rated at 70 hp, with cylinders grouped in two blocks with two cylinders each, designed and built by the Daimler Motoren Gesellschaft in Stuttgart as one of the first aircraft engines of that company. The cylinder blocks are of cast iron with integral water jacket. The pistons are forged steel. The engine was used in the Rumpler Taube.

Mercedes D III A
Germany 1916

Six-cylinder inline water cooled piston engine, rated at 161 hp, designed and built by the Daimler Motoren Gesellschaft in Stuttgart. It is fitted with a double carburettor with a duct providing hot air from oil cooled in the crankase and a decompressor, facilitating engine starting. It was used in the Albatros D.III, Albatros D.V, Pfalz D.IIIa, Pfalz D.XII, and Junkers J 10 (Cl.I).

Mercedes D IV h
Germany 1915

Eight cylinder inline water cooled piston engine, rated at 287 hp, designed and built by the Daimler Motoren Gesellschaft in Stuttgart, fitted with two carburettors, water pump and submerged oil pump. It was used in the Albatros C.V.

Mercedes D IVa
Germany 1916

Six-cylinder inline water cooled piston engine, rated at 270 hp, designed and built by the Daimler Motoren Gesellschaft in Stuttgart as F 1686. It was the successor of the unsuccessful 8 cylinder D IV in the class of 200 hp plus engines. It was used in the AEG G. IV, Albatros C.X, C.XII, Gotha G.II, G.III, G.IV, G.V, G.VII, Pfalz C.I, Rumpler C.IV, C.V, G.III, and Friedrichshafen G.III, G.IV, N.I.

Benz Bz IVd
Germany 1917

Austro – Daimler DM-200
Austria – Hungary 1916

⇧ Six-cylinder inline water cooled piston engine, rated at 200 hp, designed and built by the Austro-Daimler company. The cylinders are cast and machined from steel. The pistons are aluminum and the water jackets are welded steel. The carburettor is heated by water from the cooling system. It was used in the Lloyd C.II, Lloyd C.V, Oeffag D.III, Hannover Cl.V, and Brandenburg C.I.

⇦ Six-cylinder inline liquid cooled piston engine, rated at 255 hp. It is a modified version with aluminum pistons of the Benz Bz IV engine from 1915, of which 6,400 were built. It was used in the AEG J.I, J.II, N.I, AGO C.IV, Albatros C.VII, C.XV, G.III, J.I, Halberstadt C.V, Friedrichshafen G.II, FF 49, FF 59, DFW C.V and LVG C.V.

BMW III A
Germany 1917

NAG C III
Germany 1916

Six-cylinder inline liquid cooled piston engine, rated at 226 hp, designed and built by the Bayerische Motoren Werke in Munich. It was one of the best engines in its class – light, reliable, and providing high performance. Due to these advantages it was used in fighter aircraft such as the Fokker D.VII and Pfalz D. XII.

Six-cylinder inline water cooled piston engine, rated at 210 hp, designed by R. Conrad and built by the Nationale Automobil Gesellschaft mbH in Berlin. Technical features similar to those used in Mercedes engines were used. It was built in small numbers. It was used in the DFW C.Vc and Fokker D.VII.

Liberty 12
USA 1917

V-12 liquid cooled inline piston engine, rated at 450 hp. It was a simple and reliable design, which was possible thanks to simple design and technology. Mass production was undertaken by the Ford, Lincoln, Packard, Marmon and Buick automotive companies. Up to November 1918 20,478 engines were built. The Liberty was used for many years in civil and military aircraft, like the Airco DH-4 and DH-9A, Curtiss flying boats of the R-, H-, HS- and NC- series, NAF F-5L, Martin MB-1 and MB-2. The displayed engine is incomplete.

Rolls–Royce Eagle IX
Great Britain 1922

V-12 cylinder water cooled inline piston engine, rated at 390 hp. Studies on aircraft engines at the Rolls-Royce company began in 1914, after the British Admiralty's order for a 200 hp engine. The first type to enter series production in 1915 was the Eagle I, a 12 cylinder water cooled engine. Continuous upgrades of this design led to subsequent more powerful and reliable production versions (Eagle II, III, IV, V, VI, VII, VIII). The last military version was the Eagle VIII, rated at 360 hp at 1,800 RPM, fitted with four carburettors, one per three cylinders. After the war studies on a high power engine for civil aviation began, which resulted in the Eagle IX engine, fitted with two Claudel-Hobson carburettors and four magnetos. It was used in the Handley-Page 0/400 and Dornier Do J II Wal.

Argus As-5
Germany 1924 – 27

W-24-cylinder double-V liquid cooled piston engine, rated at 1,500 hp, designed by Dr Ing. Riedl. It was an experimental engine, envisaged for a large passenger aircraft. The Treaty of Versailles forbade Germany to build multi-engine aircraft, which resulted in the idea of building an aircraft powered by a single high power engine. The Argus As-5 engine turned out to be too heavy and thus it did not enter series production.

Rolls-Royce Kestrel II S
Great Britain 1930

V-12 cylinder liquid cooled inline piston engine, rated at 525 hp, designed in 1926 at the Rolls-Royce works as the first of the new generation of engines of that company. It was succeeded by the RR Goshawk and RR Peregrine and the larger RR Buzzard. It was used in the Hawker Hart, Demon, Fury and Nimrod, among many others.

Chapter 5: Engines

Skoda-Bristol *Pegaz* IIM2
Poland 1934

Nine cylinder air cooled radial engine, rated at 600 hp. It was built by the Polish Skoda Works in Warsaw under licence from the British Bristol company. Poland undertook licence production, despite the fact that the engine caused several problems with reduction gear overheating. It was replaced in production by the much better *Pegaz* VIIIA engine. It was used in the PZL P.23A *Karaś* (Crucian) reconnaissance and bomber aircraft.

PZL *Pegaz* VIII
Poland 1936

Nine cylinder air cooled radial piston engine, rated at 705 hp, built by the No.1 Engine Factory in Warsaw–Okęcie under licence from Bristol. It replaced in production the unsuccessful *Pegaz* II engine. During 1936-1937 over 350 *Pegaz* VIII engines were built. The *Pegaz* VIII was replaced in production by the *Pegaz* XX, intended for the PZL 37 *Łoś* (Moose) and PZL 46 *Sum* (Catfish). The *Pegaz* VIII powered the PZL 23B *Karaś* (Crucian), PZL 30 and PZL 42.

PZL *Pegaz* XX
Poland 1938

Nine cylinder air cooled radial piston engine, rated at 850 hp, built by the No.1 Engine Factory in Warsaw–Okęcie under licence from Bristol. The *Pegaz* XX powered the PZL P.37 *Łoś* (Moose) and PZL P.46 *Sum* (Catfish).

Renault 6Q11
France 1938

Six cylinder inverted inline air cooled piston engine, rated at 220 hp, designed and built by the Société Anonyme des Moteurs Renault company in Billancourt. It was used in the Caudron-Renault C-445 *Goeland* and Caudron-Renault C-635 *Simoun*.

Polish Aviation Museum Cracow

Wright R-975-C4 Whirlwind J-6
USA 1933

Nine cylinder air cooled radial piston engine, rated at 400 hp. The Whirlwind proved to be an exceptionally successful design. In 1927 Charles Lindbergh made the first non-stop flight over the Atlantic from New York to Paris in the Ryan NYP "Spirit of St Louis", powered by a J-5C Whirlwind engine. In the '30s these engines were licence built in Poland by the Polish Skoda and Avia companies. Whirlwinds (5, 7, and 9 cylinder versions) powered training, observation and executive aircraft, airships, and even tanks and self-propelled guns. During World War II Whirlwinds were licence-built by the Continental company, due to excessive demand for higher power Wright engines.

Alfa-Romeo 126 RC 34
Italy 1934

Alfa Romeo built under British licence Bristol Jupiter and Pegasus engines and based some of their own designs on them. The Alfa-Romeo 126 RC 34 is a 9-cylinder air cooled radial piston engine, rated at 780 hp. It is a development version of the Bristol Pegasus engine. It was used in most Italian World War II bombers, like the CANT Z.506 *Airone*, Savoia SM-73, SM-74, SM-79 *Sparviero*, SM-81 *Pipistrello*, Caproni Bergamaschi AP-1 and also the Junkers Ju 52.

BMW-801 D2
Germany 1941

14-cylinder air cooled piston twin-row radial engine, designed at the Bayerische Motoren Werke in Munich. The engine has direct fuel injection and two speed supercharger as well as so called *Kommando* gear, an automatic device controlling the engine and propeller pitch, which facilitated piloting the aircraft. Another significant feature is forced air cooling by a fan mounted in front of the engine. The BMW-801 was built in large numbers and used in the Focke-Wulf Fw 190 A-3 to A-9 fighters, Junkers Ju 88 G and H, Junkers Ju 188 E, F and Junkers Ju 290 bombers.

Pratt & Whitney R-1830-S3C4-4
USA 1939

14-cylinder air cooled twin-row radial engine, rated at 1,200 hp, designed at the Pratt & Whitney plant in East Hartford, Connecticut, USA. It is the most numerous radial engine built in the history of aviation. Production started in 1934. The displayed engine represents the first version with two speed supercharger, introduced in 1939. This increased the ability of the engine to be used on aircraft operating at higher altitudes. The engine powered the F4F Wildcat, Vickers Wellington IV, Douglas A20 Havoc, Douglas C-47B Dakota and Bristol Beaufort amongst others.

CHAPTER 5: ENGINES

WRIGHT R-2600-23 CYCLONE 14
USA 1942

14-cylinder air cooled twin-row radial piston engine fitted with a single stage, two speed supercharger with a hydraulic clutch, rated at 1,600 hp. It was a development version of the single row R-1820 Cyclone and was also called Twin Cyclone. The engine was built in large numbers (ca. 50,000) by the Wright Aeronautical Corporation and was used by many notable American World War II aircraft like the Douglas A-20 Boston, North American B-25 Mitchell, Curtiss SB2C Helldiver, Grumman TBF Avenger, Martin Mariner, Martin Baltimore.

DAIMLER–BENZ DB 600 G
Germany 1936

12-cylinder liquid cooled inverted V inline piston engine, rated at 950 hp, designed by Dr Berger at the Daimler-Benz plant in 1935. The DB 600 was the first of the DB 601, DB 603 and DB 605 engine series, well known during World War II and licence built in Japan and Italy. The characteristic feature of the 12-cylinder DB engines was the provision for a cannon between the cylinder blocks.

Although the DB 600 was primarily destined for fighter aircraft, it was used also in other types of military aircraft. The displayed DB 600G version, fitted with the 3-nozzle carburettor, was designed in 1936. 2,281 DB 600 engines were built. The DB 600 powered the Heinkel He 111D, F, G and Dornier Do 17S bombers.

JUNKERS JUMO 211
Germany 1936

12-cylinder liquid cooled inverted V inline piston engine rated at 1,200 hp, with direct fuel injection and two-speed supercharger, boosting the power at higher altitudes. Fuel injection was the most important of the innovative technical features, increasing the performance and handling qualities of the engine.

The Jumo 211 engine was designed by a team led by Professor Hugo Junkers. Several versions of the engine were built in large numbers throughout World War II. Production totalled about 68,000 examples. The Jumo 211 powered the most versions of the Heinkel He 111 and Junkers Ju 88 bombers, and the Junkers Ju 87 dive bomber.

ROLLS–ROYCE MERLIN Mk XX
Great Britain 1940

V-12 liquid (ethylene glycol) cooled inline piston engine, rated at 1,300 hp, with a single stage two-speed supercharger and reduction gear. It is a version of the most famous Rolls-Royce piston engine. Various versions of Merlin engines powered the Hawker Hurricane, Supermarine Spitfire, de Havilland Mosquito, Avro Lancaster, Handley Page Halifax, Fairey Battle, Fairey Barracuda and many other aircraft. 168,040 Merlin engines were built, among them 28,021 of the Mk XX version. Versions licence-built in USA by the Packard company were used in the Curtiss P-40 Kittyhawk, North American P-51 Mustang and Supermarine Spitfire Mk XVI fighters. The Merlin Mk XX version powered the Avro Lancaster Mk I, III, VII, Boulton & Paul Defiant Mk II and Bristol Beaufighter Mk II aircraft.

POLISH AVIATION MUSEUM CRACOW

Bristol Siddeley Hercules 264
Great Britain 1949

14-cylinder air cooled twin-row radial piston engine, rated at 1,950 hp. A version of the most famous Bristol sleeve-valve piston engine. During 1938-1966 130,000 Hercules engines of various versions were built. During World War II Bristol Hercules engines powered the Bristol Beaufighter, Short Stirling, Short Sunderland, Saro Lerwick, Handley Page Halifax and Vickers Wellington aircraft. The Hercules 264 was the powerplant of the Vickers Varsity Mk I transport aircraft.

Junkers Jumo 205D
Germany 1940

Six cylinder inline two stroke liquid cooled diesel engine, rated at 880 hp. The engine has two opposed pistons working in each cylinder, two crankshafts and a blower providing air to the cylinders. This system was patented by Prof. Hugo Junkers in 1907 and realized for the first time in 1926. The Jumo 205D engine was used in the Dornier Do 26 and Blohm & Voss BV 138 flying boats.

Bramo 323 A Fafnir
Germany 1937

Nine cylinder air cooled radial piston engine, rated at 900 hp, with steel cylinders and aluminum cylinder heads, fitted with a supercharger and fuel injection. The engine was designed at the Brandenburgische Motorenwerke company in Berlin, which was established by Siemens GmbH in 1936 and took over the Siemens' aircraft engine division. It was used in the Dornier Do 17, Do 19 and Do 24T.

P.Z.Inż Major Typ 4
Poland 1935

Four cylinder air cooled inverted inline piston engine, rated at 120 hp, built by the National Engineering Works in Ursus near Warsaw. It was used in the RWD-13 aircraft. Production totalled about 100 examples.

The displayed engine was installed in the RWD-13 aircraft with the registration SP-BML, famous through the daring escape from Gdynia, besieged by the Germans, to Sweden on September 14th, 1939. The aircraft was interned in Sweden until the end of the war. In 1952 it had an accident. In 1998 a Swedish pilot, Viking Österlindh, donated the surviving engine to the Polish Aviation Museum.

Shvetsov Ash-21

USSR

Seven cylinder air cooled radial piston engine, rated at 700 hp, with direct fuel injection. Designed by a team led by A. Shvetsov. The engine was produced after the Second World War in the USSR and under licence in Czechoslovakia as the M-21. It was the powerplant of the UTB and Yak-11 training aircraft.

Argus As – 10c

Germany 1932

Eight cylinder air cooled inverted V inline piston engine, rated at 240 KM, designed at the Argus Motoren Gesellschaft company in 1932. It was a very successful design. Series production began in 1934, and around 10,000 engines were built by 1939. It was used in the Fieseler Fi 156 *Storch*, Arado Ar 66, Focke-Wulf Fw 58 *Weihe* and Messerschmitt Bf 108 *Taifun*.

Mikulin M-34

USSR 1933

V-12 water cooled inline piston engine, rated at 850 hp, fitted with a centrifugal supercharger, designed by a team led by A. Mikulin in 1931. In the following years many modifications were applied, like the reduction gear, metal variable-pitch propeller, refined supercharger and other technology and design changes, increasing the power of the engine. On the basis of the M-34 the AM-35A, AM-38, AM-42 engines, used in various famous World War II aircraft, were designed.

Heavy weight meant that the engine was suitable only for large aircraft. It powered the TB-3 bomber.

Hispano-Suiza H Typ 82

France 1938

24-cylinder liquid cooled H-Type inline engine, rated at 2,000 hp. A prototype of an engine with four cylinder blocks with six cylinders in each and two superchargers. It did not enter series production due to complicated construction. The only production H-type engine was the British Napier Sabre, used in the Hawker Typhoon and Tempest fighters during the Second World War.

AM-38F
USSR 1943

V-12 liquid cooled inline piston engine with a floatless carburettor and supercharger, designed by the team led by A. Mikulin, as a further development of the AM-35 engine. The AM-38F is a more powerful version, rated at 1,750 hp. It was built in large numbers and used in the Il-2 attack aircraft. Some MiG-3 fighters were also retrofitted with AM-38 engines.

Klimov VK-105PF
USSR 1942

V-12 liquid cooled inline piston engine, rated at 1,300 hp, designed by a team led by V. Klimov. It was a development of the French Hispano-Suiza engine, licence-built in the USSR. The VK-105 engine is fitted with six carburetors, one per every two cylinders, and a two speed supercharger. A cannon, firing through the propeller shaft, could be placed between the cylinder rows. It was used in the Yak-1, Yak-3, Yak-9 and Yak-9M fighters and the SB and Pe-2 bombers, amongst others.

Shvetsov ASh-82FN
USSR 1943

14-cylinder air cooled twin-row radial piston engine, rated at 1,850 hp, designed by a team led by A. Shvetsov. The engine was developed as a result of experience gained during the Civil War in Spain, which revealed that a small size high power air cooled engine was needed. In 1942 the M-82, fitted with a floatless carburetor, entered production. In 1943 the production of the ASh-82FN fuel injected version began. The engine powered the Tu-2, La-5FN, La-7, Pe-8 and Il-12 aircraft.

LiT-3
Poland 1957

Seven cylinder air cooled radial piston engine with a single-stage supercharger, rated at 575 hp, specified for helicopters. It is Soviet Ivchenko AI-26W engine, licence built in Poland by PZL Rzeszów. In the mid 1950s Poland purchased the licence for the Mi-1 helicopter and its engine.

The engine is fitted with a bevel gear transmission assembly, driving the main and tail rotors, a clutch for smooth coupling and decoupling the engine with the rotors and a cooling fan. Compressed air is used for engine startup. It was the powerplant of the SM-1 (licence-built Mi-1) and SM-2 helicopters.

WN-3
Poland 1952

Seven cylinder air cooled radial piston engine, rated at 320 hp, with no supercharger and propeller reduction gear. Compressed air is used for engine startup. Designed by a team leb by W. Narkiewicz for a training aircraft designed by T. Sołtyk's team. It was the further development of the earlier WN-2. The WN-3 was the first engine of Polish design which entered series production after World War II. It was the powerplant of the TS-8 *Bies* (Devil) and MD-12 aircraft.

RD-10A
USSR 1946

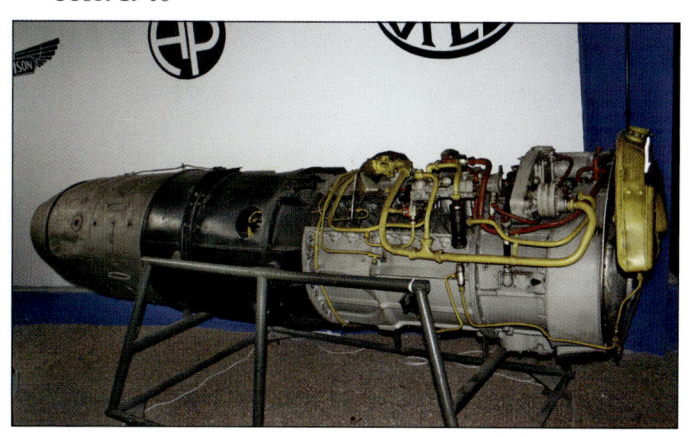

Axial-flow turbojet engine, rated at 8.83 kN. It is an improved Soviet copy of the German Junkers Jumo 004 engine, used during the Second World War in the Messerschmitt Me 262 *Schwalbe* fighter and Arado Ar 234 *Blitz* reconnaissance and bomber aircraft. After the war production of the Junkers engine was moved from Dessau to Ufa in the USSR. Modifications increasing thrust and durability were developed by the Klimov Design Bureau. The RD-10A powered the Yak-17W jet trainer

Lis-5
Poland 1956

Centrifugal-flow turbojet engine, rated at 33 kN of thrust with afterburner. It is a licence-built version of the Soviet VK-1F engine, used in the MiG-17, built in Poland by WSK Rzeszów. Poland purchased the licence for MiG-17 and VK-1F engines. The Soviet original is a development version of the VK-1A engine from the MiG-15*bis*, fitted with afterburner. The VK-1A was based on the Rolls-Royce Nene II engine. In Poland the Lis-5 engines were built from 1956 to 1984. They were used in the Lim-5 (MiG-17F), Lim-5P (MiG-17PF), Lim-6M, Lim-6*bis*.

SO-1
Poland 1964

Axial-flow turbojet engine, rated at 9.8 kN, designed entirely in Poland at the Aviation Institute for the TS-11 *Iskra* (Spark) jet trainer. After some technical problems had been solved, production commenced in 1968 and totalled 700 engines. Its development version was the SO-3, mounted in later versions of the *Iskra* and retrofitted to earlier versions during overhauls.

Lyulka AL-7

USSR 1959

Axial-flow turbojet engine, rated at 96 kN of thrust with afterburner, designed at the Saturn Design Bureau under the supervision of Archip Lyulka. The engine was intended for supersonic aircraft, although it was more suitable for bombers and transport aircraft. Despite this fact it became the powerplant of the Su-7 fighter bomber. Its main drawback was extremely high fuel consumption, which greatly reduced the Su-7's range and weapons load. The AL-7 is the largest jet engine in the Museum's collection.

Ivchenko AI-25

USSR 1966

Twin-shaft medium bypass turbofan engine, rated at 14.7 kN, designed in the mid 1960s at the Ivchenko Design Bureau for the Yakovlev Yak-40. Engines of the AI-25 family also powered the Czechoslovak Aero L-39 *Albatros* trainer, operated by most Warsaw Pact member countries and the Polish-Soviet M-15 *Belphegor* agricultural aircraft. The development version is the AI-25TL. The AI-25 was also a starting point for the Lotarev DV-2 engine built in Slovakia.

V-2 (A-4)

Germany 1942

Liquid fuel (alcohol/liquid oxygen) rocket engine, rated at 25 tons of thrust, designed by Walter Thiel, used in the A-4/V-2 rocket, designed by Wernher von Braun. The V-2 (*Vergeltungswaffe* - 2, revenge weapon 2) was the first ballistic missile used in combat. The Germans used V-2 missiles against London and other Allied cities during the final period of the Second World War. The Museum possesses three elements of the V-2 engine – the steam generator, which produced steam that drove the fuel pump, the fuel pump and engine.

Armstrong Siddeley Viper

The Viper is a turbojet engine rated at 11.1 kN (2,472 lb), designed and produced by the British Armstrong Siddeley company in 1951, and then by Bristol Siddeley and Rolls-Royce. The design is based on the Armstrong Siddeley Sapphire engine. It was initially developed as an expendable engine for the GAF Jindivik target drone, but then production of engines made of standard materials began. The Vipers were primarily used in trainer aircraft, like the BAC Jet Provost, Aermacchi MB-326 and MB-339, attack BAC Strikemaster and executive Hawker Siddeley Dominie. Engines licence-built in Yugoslavia powered the SOKO G-2 *Galeb*, G-4 *Super Galeb* and Soko J-22 *Orao* aircraft. The first prototype of Polish TS-11 *Iskra* trainer was powered by a Viper 8 engine, purchased in Yugoslavia.